The Stone of Destiny & The Scots

The Stone's Journey to Perth Museum

John Hulbert

Illustrations by Rob Hands

TIPPERMUIR
· BOOKS LIMITED ·

The Stone of Destiny & The Scots – John Hulbert Copyright © 2024. All rights reserved.

The right of John Hulbert to be identified as the author of the Work has been asserted in accordance with the Copyright, Designs & Patents Act 1988.

This first edition published and copyright 2024 by
Tippermuir Books Ltd, Perth, Scotland.

mail@tippermuirbooks.co.uk – www.tippermuirbooks.co.uk.

ISBN 978-1-913836-17-7 (paperback).

A CIP catalogue record for this book is available from the British Library.

Project coordination and editorial by Paul S Philippou.

Cover design by Matthew Mackie.

Editorial support: Ajay Close, Steve Zajda and Jean Hands.

Co-founders and publishers of Tippermuir Books:
Rob Hands, Matthew Mackie and Paul S Philippou.

Text design, layout, and artwork by Bernard Chandler [graffik].
Text set in Dante MT Std Regular 10.8/14pt with Dante MT Std Bold titling.

Printed and bound by Ashford Colour Press.

For Sara

Also by John Hulbert

Perth: A Comprehensive Guide for Locals and Visitors
This is the first comprehensive guide to the ancient city of Perth. Closely examining each area of the city, John Hubert explores the institutions, trades, traditions and people that have contributed of Perth's development from the earliest settlement on the site through to the present day. Complete with full colour photographs and maps, the guide provides a detailed overview of Perth's history and its role in wider Scottish and international contexts. It is also an excellent celebration of the city's architecture and public art.

John Hubert's guide to Perth is a magnificent combination of historic analysis and contemporary appreciation of our fine city. It is an invaluable book, written with such care and precision by a former Provost. **John Swinney MSP**

Suitable for lifelong Perth dwellers and first time visitors, Dr Hulbert's book leads the reader through Perth, acting as an invisible tour guide and expanding on the historic detail on the city's streets. Inquisitive individuals want to understand the why's and what's of their subject. Why is Perth here? What significant events in its history impinge on its present situation? What are Perth's important streets and how did they develop? What about its art and architecture? How did its distinctive traditions and institutions arise? And above all, who were its famous sons and daughters? **The Courier**

Former Provost's Labour of Love. John Hulbert's fondness and fascination for the Fair City is reflected in this newly published guide book. This well-received addition to the library of books on Perth features hundreds of fine photographs. **Perthshire Advertiser**

Nearly 20 years' experience on Perth & Kinross Council, including five as Provost mean Hulbert's knowledge and experience stood him in good stead for this book. Valuable for locals and visitors alike. **Scots Magazine**

Each area of the city is closely examined, and John Hulbert's deep passion for the city shines through this practical guide. **Scottish Field**

This is a truly magnificent guide to Perth, with hundreds of colour pictures of the places to see, visit and enjoy. Unlike standard guides, here one can feel the pride and pain of a writer who loves his city. John Hulbert's book gives much more than facts and a list of places, but a powerful warmth and feeling for Perth. **Stramash**

Scotland's Oldest and Newest City:
How Perth Regained its City Status and Why it Matters

What was the biggest challenge to Perth becoming a city again? Why was Perth once more important than Edinburgh? How exactly did Perth execute its successful campaign for city status? All of this and more is revealed in John Hulbert's account of how Perth became a city once again. Former Provost of Perth & Kinross, and leader of Perth's campaign, Hulbert is the ideal person to tell the inside story of the tactics deployed to achieve the restoration of Perth's City Status, the most important event in Perth's history in nearly 200 years. Beginning with Perth's history as the ancient capital city of Scotland and tracing its pre-eminence amongst Scottish Royal Burghs, this book explores Perth's loss of city status in 1975 and the development of the city status application strategy. Culminating in Perth's eventual success, this is the story of how its citizens fought to regain its former glory against the odds in 2012. Rich with local and national history, and with chapters looking forward to the future of Perth, this book, complete with beautiful colour photographs, will appeal to historians, visitors and Perth locals alike.

In this book former Provost Dr John Hulbert reveals how despite the enormous odds stacked against it the Fair City's claim prevailed. Rich with local and national history, and with chapters looking forward to the future of Perth, the book, complete with colour photographs, will appeal to historians, visitors and locals alike. **The Courier**

Former Provost of Perth & Kinross and leader of Perth's campaign, John Hulbert begins with Perth's history as the ancient capital of Scotland and traces its pre-eminence amongst Scottish Royal Burghs. He then explores its loss of city status in 1975, and the development of the city status application strategy. Culminating in Perth's eventual success, this is the story of how its citizens fought to regain its former glory, finally winning against the odds in 2012.
The Weekend Courier

It is the sections on the sheer scale of activity in the run up to the contest where John Hulbert brings the campaign to life. The engaging of Scotland's wider political community and the co-operation that was secured are also recognised as key factors in Perth's eventual success. **Pete Wishart MP**

The former Provost of Perth & Kinross, Dr John Hulbert, is the ideal person to tell the inside story of Perth's campaign to restore its City status. This new work asks and answers questions such as What was the biggest challenge to Perth becoming a city again? Why was Perth more important than Edinburgh? And how exactly did Perth execute its successful campaign against the enormous odds stacked against it? Bringing new opportunities and funding streams, becoming a city once more in 2012 was hailed as the most important event in the history of Perth for nearly 200 years. **Perthshire Advertiser**

About the Author

Dr John Hulbert was brought up in St Andrews and studied medicine in Edinburgh. He worked first in medical research and then was a GP for over 30 years. He lives with his wife, Sara, in the Perthshire village of Longforgan.

Elected to Perth & Kinross Council in 1995, he served as Provost from 2007 to 2012. As Provost, he co-ordinated Perth's 800th anniversary celebrations in 2010, and led the successful endeavour to restore Perth's city status which had been unjustly removed in 1975. He described that campaign in his 2016 book, *Scotland's Oldest & Newest City: How Perth regained its city status and why it matters.* Drawing on the knowledge he had gained as Provost, he also published *Perth: A Comprehensive Guide for Locals and Visitors* in 2014. It was the first illustrated guide book for Perth.

He is active in several Perth organisations, being chairman of the Friends of St John's Kirk, an Honorary Fellow of the Royal Scottish Geographical Society, an Honorary Friend of the Black Watch Castle and Museum, and an Officer of the Order of St John. In 2012, the President of Poland awarded Dr Hulbert the Knights Cross of the Order of Merit of the Republic of Poland, in recognition of his work developing good relations between Perth and Poland.

In Longforgan, he is active in the Parish church, where he has been an elder for many years, and with his wife, Sara, he has established an orchard of ancient varieties of Scottish pear trees, which is recognised by the Plant Heritage Society as a 'National Collection'.

Acknowledgements

The inspiration to write this book dawned slowly as two contrasting developments became apparent. The first was that Perth was to be granted the opportunity to display the Stone of Destiny in its new museum. Secondly, on rereading the history of the Stone, I became convinced of the threadbare nature of the usual explanation for the local origin of the Stone. This was that following his defeat of the Picts in 843, King Kenneth MacAlpin discarded the ancient Irish Stone in favour of a Pictish icon in order to appease the wounded sentiments of the defeated Picts. The only alternative explanation for the local origin of the Stone, that it had been concealed from Edward's soldiers by the monks of Scone Abbey, was not entertained by those charged with displaying the Stone in Edinburgh and overseeing its move to Perth. Nevertheless there were a number of amateur historians, who over the last 100 years, raised well-founded doubts. Their testimony intrigued me, and I am greatly indebted to them. They are all acknowledged in the book.

A second source of inspiration was the publication of the book *The Scots: A Genetic Journey* by Alistair Moffat and James F Wilson. For the first time, this book provided evidence that the account of the origin of The Scots in the Declaration of Arbroath was not all 'myth and fable' as claimed by Victorian historians. I corresponded with Professor Wilson about the westward migration of the Yamnaya peoples of the Steppes, and I am grateful to him for sharing his knowledge.

As one who had recently begun to learn Gaelic, I was especially interested in the linguistic evidence, although it is still controversial. Gaelic and Viking place names are important historical markers. I was fortunate to be able to consult the Gaelic scholar Ian MacIlleChiar on the linguistic background to the names that have been associated with the castle now known as Dunstaffnage, and also on Gaelic generally.

I want to acknowledge the help and unstinting support I have always had from the staff at Perth's A K Bell Library. No author involved in historical research could have been better served.

Finally, I want to thank my dear wife, Sara, who has provided help and encouragement at all times. Her critical eye, intuitive suggestions and meticulous proofreading have been very important in bringing this project to fruition. It is with great gratitude that I dedicate this book to her.

John Hulbert

CONTENTS

Foreword
by Brigadier Sir Melville Jameson KCVO, CBE, CSt

The mystery of the Stone of Destiny also known as the Stone of Scone lives on. This book is a detailed and intriguing account of its history; it clearly lays out the many different fascinating myths and legends surrounding this iconic stone. *Was it really Jacob's Pillow or the Pharaoh's Stone or perhaps even St Columba's Pillow on Iona? Did it make the journey all the way from Egypt with Pharaoh's daughter Scota and The Scots tribe to Spain and thence to Ireland in 500 and Scotland 1,000 years later?*

The book highlights how the Stone was moved to Iona during the time of St Columba and thence to Scone around 800, and how it survived those turbulent years in Scotland when despite Viking invasions and wars between the Picts and The Scots, 29 Scottish kings were crowned/enthroned on the Stone.

There is much debate outlined in this book about whether the stone, captured by King Edward I of England in 1296, is in fact the original one or was it substituted by the brave monks of Scone Abbey. If so, despite various searches, it has never been found.

Then the author tells the story that after 700 years peacefully lying in state at Westminster Abbey in the Coronation Chair, in 1950, the Stone was covertly removed and hidden by four Glasgow students, led by Ian Hamilton, which took everyone by surprise; it was eventually found at Arbroath Abbey.

More recently, however, in 1996, it was decided by the John Major government 'out of the blue' that it should be returned to Scotland, but it would continue to be used for coronations in Westminster. Hastily, it was decided it should be placed in Edinburgh Castle beside the Crown Jewels of Scotland – not a particularly fitting place for this iconic stone and it was still some way from home. This year, 2023, under heavy guard, it made the journey south to Westminster Abbey for the coronation of King Charles III.

The writing of this book is timely indeed. Following this extraordinary history over 3,000 years, a powerful campaign was launched from the city of Perth to return the Stone of Destiny to Perthshire, to its rightful home. After some lengthy deliberation, it was decided by the

Commissioners of Regalia in Edinburgh that the Stone should come home. So, from 2024, its final resting place is in the new museum of Perth.

Brigadier Sir Melville Jamieson KCVO, CBE, CSt
Lord Lieutenant of Perth & Kinross, 2006–20,
Chief Executive Royal Edinburgh Military Tattoo, 1995–2007
June 2023

Notes on the Text

All dates in the book are 'AD/Common Era' unless otherwise stated.

Over the centuries the Stone of Destiny has been known by a variety of other names: Jacob's Pillow, the Pharaoh's Stone, the Eastern Stone, the Coronation Stone and the Stone of Scone, and this can cause confusion. If the stone uplifted by Edward's troops was indeed a substitute, then clearly the term, the Stone of Destiny should refer to the original stone brought to Scone from Argyll, and the stone used for the coronation of Charles III should be called the Stone of Scone, because that is certainly its origin. The modern stone, however, is universally called the Stone of Destiny in the media, and in books, pamphlets and descriptions of it in Edinburgh and Perth, and so in this book a pragmatic approach has been taken. The term the Stone of Destiny is used to describe the stone at all stages of its history, and the particular manifestation of the stone is clarified by the context, and sometimes by additional adjectives.

There can also be confusion with the term 'Scots'. According to legend the Stone of Destiny belonged to a Middle Eastern clan which was descended from Scota, the daughter of a Pharaoh. The name of the clan, derived from their matriarch was 'The Scots', and their king was known as the King of The Scots. The ancient chronicles tell us that this clan brought the Stone from Spain to Ireland, and then to Argyll. When referring to this clan, I have used the term 'The Scots', giving a capital 'T' to the definite article.

The Top Face of the
Stone of Destiny

POINTS TO NOTE

The countersunk rings.

....

The rectangular groove on the surface and the
additional groove on the right hand side.

....

The faint saltire on the top left hand corner.

....

The more marked regular cross in the centre of the top border.

....

The line of the repair beginning to the right of the
regular cross in the top border and curving down
towards the lower right hand corner.

....

The broken corners and general rough,
worn appearance of the Stone of Destiny.

Introduction
The Stone of Destiny and The Scots

REVERED CEREMONIAL OBJECTS are often carved, painted, or otherwise decorated, and are invariably clean and polished. Sometimes they are beautiful, and always they show evidence of care and attention. The Stone of Destiny has none of these attributes. Uniquely, it is rough and dusty; clumsily cut down in size; chipped, broken and crudely repaired; coarsely carved on one surface and with utilitarian iron fixings attached to each end. And yet, more than 700 years ago it was considered to be an object of supreme civic importance by an invading superpower; a century and more ago it was perceived to be a religious relic and was imbued with reverence, even sanctity; and still today it rouses interest and passion, which is manifest by the pomp and ceremony, more appropriate to a head of State, which has been accorded to it recently.

In December 2020, it was announced that the Stone of Destiny was to be returned to Perthshire to be the centrepiece of the new Perth Museum. In this location, the Stone of Destiny is as near as it is possible to be to its historical location in Scone Abbey, adjacent to Moot Hill. This is as it should be. The Stone of Destiny belongs to Scotland. In the absence of the Abbey building in Old Scone, the right place for it to be is in the centre of Perth where it can be kept secure and put on display.

For 1,500 years, and perhaps for very much longer, the Stone of Destiny has been inextricably linked with Scotland and The Scots. The story of this connection includes historical fact, legend and myth, but is so compounded by *non sequiturs*, gaps, contradictions and a variety of explanations, that it is quite difficult to identify the facts and work out the probable sequence of events.

There are several eras in the legendary history of the Stone of Destiny, each of which is important in understanding the attitude towards it at the present time. The first is what one might call its 'Biblical' history, beginning with a fanciful myth that the Stone of Destiny was Jacob's Pillow in the Old Testament account of Jacob's dream in which God promised that he would be the father of a glorious nation. Just as unlikely, but of interest, nevertheless, is another legend, involving Biblical characters, but not recorded in the Bible. It is the story that Moses gave the Stone of Destiny to Gaythelos, a Greek nobleman who married Scota, the daughter of a Pharaoh, and that she was the legendary progenitor of the tribe that bore her name, 'The Scots'.

The legends record that The Scots travelled from Egypt to an area north of the Black Sea called Scythia, which comprises the modern countries of Ukraine and Romania, and part of the Russian Federation. Then they migrated, over a period of many centuries, westwards to the north of what is now Italy, and from thence down the east coast of Italy to North Africa. They progressed along the coast of North Africa and through the Straits of Gibraltar into the Iberian Peninsula and settled for as long as 1,000 years in the area in the northwest of Spain, now known as Galicia, before invading and conquering Ireland. There is evidence that this last move is an actual historical event, occurring around 500 BC, and it is referred to in the preamble to the Declaration of Arbroath. During their time in Galicia, there is the first reference in the various medieval chronicles of a sacred stone, which was used by the King of The Scots in Spain for inaugurations and as a seat of justice.

In mediaeval times, enthroning or inauguration, rather than crowning was the way that Celtic peoples confirmed the assumption of power and responsibility by a new king. In Scotland, the Stone of Destiny was the throne used for this purpose.

Once The Scots had invaded Ireland, legends continue to refer to a stone upon which inaugurations took place, but with conflicting accounts of its origin. Then in the fourth and fifth centuries, the people in the northeast of Ireland began to filter across the North Channel and settle in what is now Argyll. Gradually this settlement developed and the ties between it and Ireland weakened.

The next stage in the story of the Stone of Destiny tells of its removal from Ireland to Scotland. That an 'inaugural stone' which was used to confirm the authority and responsibilities of a new king, came from Ireland to mainland Scotland during the sixth century, seems fairly certain. It was moved for a time to Iona, where it was probably used by St Columba to inaugurate King Àedàn in 574. Later, after Columba's death, the danger of Viking raids necessitated its return to mainland Scotland for safekeeping, perhaps to the keep at Dun Monaidh on the site now occupied by the Castle of Dunstaffnage, north of Oban. Information about the Stone of Destiny at this time is scanty, but it was probably taken to the fortress of the kings of Dàl Riada on Dunadd, a volcanic outcrop piercing through the marshy flood plain of the River Add, a few miles east of the modern village of Crinan.

At that time (from around 300 to 840), Scotland from the central belt northwards was divided between The Scots, who ruled in Argyll, and the more numerous Picts who were dominant in the rest of Scotland from the Forth to the Pentland Firth, and west to the Inner Hebrides. The Picts and Scots were regularly at war with each other, with dominance swaying from east to west and back, and complicated by regular intermarriage between the royal households. At the end of this period, during the reign in Argyll of King Kenneth MacAlpin, the dominant province of Pictland was Fortriu, which comprised most of the traditional county of Perthshire including Menteith, and its centre was at Scone.

In 843, Kenneth MacAlpin, the King of The Scots of Dàl Riada, over-whelmed the Picts, and massacred their nobility. He then moved his royal base from Argyll to Scone to consolidate his authority over the whole of Pictland, and rule over the nascent oldest, still-existing, nation state in Europe. The legends record that, in due course, MacAlpin brought the Stone of Destiny to Scone, where it was eventually installed in Scone Abbey. Here the Stone of Destiny was kept securely in the care of the Augustinian monks who took it outside the abbey for the inaugurations of MacAlpin's successors as the kings of Scots – perhaps as many as 29 of them, up to and including John Balliol in 1292.

The last period in the history of the Stone of Destiny is the most fully documented, although still replete with controversy, and brings us from the end of the thirteenth century to the present day. The year 1296 was when Edward I of England surged through Scotland leaving a trail of death and destruction. He forced the abdication of King John Balliol, and ordered his troops to confiscate the Honours of Scotland (the Crown, Sceptre and the Sword of State), the Black Rood of St Margaret as well as rings, robes and much jewellery and silver, and importantly a huge quantity of State and monastic records, most of which were never recovered. They also uplifted a stone, which they believed to be Scotland's Stone of Destiny, and took it to London. There it was incorporated into a specially-built throne in Westminster Abbey, and has been part of every coronation of the kings and queens of England and later of the United Kingdom since then.

The most important and persistent controversial narrative about the Stone of Destiny is the claim that prior to the raid on Scone, the ancient royal stone was spirited away by the monks of the Abbey and hidden, and replaced by a block of local sandstone. This accounts for the fact that the stone which Edward looted is indisputably a block of Devonian Old Red Sandstone, quarried at Kincarrathie, about a mile from Scone Abbey, and not a block of ancient black marble or basalt from Ireland, or indeed from further afield, as recounted in various chronicles.

There is, however, an alternative theory promoted by a reputable body of academic opinion to explain how it is that this ancient stone, revered by the Gaelic-speaking tribe from Argyll, could have been sourced from Scone. The hypothesis is that, whether or not there was a sacred stone back in Argyll, the Stone of Destiny was in fact a Pictish royal inaugural stone, that had been used by the Picts to inaugurate generations of their own kings, before their defeat by MacAlpin. The theory is that MacAlpin chose to take over an existing Pictish icon, and to assimilate an established Pictish custom, in order to facilitate the integration of the Picts into the Gaelic culture of the victorious Scots.

This book argues that there must be two Stones of Destiny – an ancient 'Irish' one imported to Argyll for the inauguration of Fergus Mòr mac Eric in 500, and a local stone, quarried from Kincarrathie, and either pressed into National Service by Kenneth MacAlpin in 843, or substituted by Abbott Henry and the monks of Scone Abbey in 1296. An attempt will be made to tease out these possibilities and to find out what happened to the 'Irish' stone,

For more than 650 years, from 1296 to 1950, the Stone of Destiny, whatever its origin, was housed in Westminster Abbey, awakening every now and then for a coronation. It is the only period in the history of the Stone about which there is absolutely no controversy. The only time the Stone left the Abbey was in 1657 when it was moved to Westminster Hall for the 'coronation' of Oliver Cromwell – a king in all but name.

Then, early on Christmas Day, 1950, in the famous raid on Westminster Abbey by four Glasgow students, the Stone of Destiny was 'clandestinely removed' to quote the careful words of the Attorney General in his

Parliamentary report about the incident, and returned to Scotland. There followed four months of hectic police activity, without result, before the Stone was deposited in Arbroath Abbey at the time of the anniversary of the Declaration of Arbroath.

Another rumour then arose that the stone left in Arbroath Abbey was not the Stone of Destiny uplifted for Edward I, but a copy made by Bailie Robert Gray, a Glasgow councillor and monumental stonemason who had been involved with the students in the famous raid. Gray certainly had the skills and the opportunity to make a copy of the Stone of Destiny. However, it has been possible for experts to examine both stones – the one in Westminster, and Bailie Gray's copy – and there is no doubt that Edward's stone went back Westminster in 1951, where it remained until 1996. In that year, the 700th anniversary of Edward's raid, it was returned to Edinburgh. In 2023, it was transported back to London for the coronation of Charles III and thereafter, returned to Scotland to be installed in its new home as the centrepiece of the new Perth Museum, established in the former Perth City Hall. There it will be adjacent to the ancient St John's Kirk, the only surviving mediaeval building in Perth and the scene of some of Scotland's most important historical events.

This book seeks to set down what is incontrovertible about the Stone of Destiny, to outline what is known about its history and the history of The Scots, and to retell some of the important events in the stone's long story leading to its permanent return to Scotland on St Andrew's Day, 1996, after an absence of 700 years, and its installation in Perth's new museum in 2024. Although, it cannot be proved conclusively that Edward I was deceived by the monks of Scone Abbey, this book argues why it is difficult to believe that the stone previously in Edinburgh was the one used for centuries before 1296 to inaugurate Kenneth MacAlpin's successors as the kings of Scots. If Abbott Henry and his monks did indeed spirit away the original Stone of Destiny, the exciting corollary is that it must be lying hidden somewhere, possibly in Perthshire, and the hope is that it will be discovered one day.

Chapter 1
Scotland's Stone of Destiny Described

THE STONE OF DESTINY is an unprepossessing object for an item of such historic and cultural importance. It is a rough block of pinkish sandstone measuring 670 mm by 420 mm by 265 mm and weighing 152 kg. It is roughly dressed; the top and sides finished to a higher standard than the bottom and end faces.

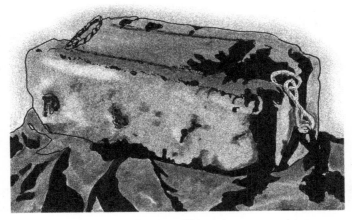

The Stone of Destiny.

The top face of the Stone of Destiny has been dressed quite smoothly.[1] However, hollows have been dug out of its surface to enable iron rings and their attached figure of eight links to be countersunk in to the stone, and present a flat surface. A rectangular groove has been cut around the top surface impinging on the pits for the rings, and there is an additional groove cut at one end. On the top surface of the stone, between the groove and the stone's edge, experts have identified what looks like two rough crosses. A very faint saltire-shaped cross can be made out close to the right-hand lower corner and in the centre of the lower border there is a more definite cross, with its long axis in-line with the stone. It is difficult

---

1 'Top', 'bottom', 'front', 'back', left' and 'right' all refer to the faces of the Stone of Destiny as seen when it was housed in the throne in Westminster Abbey.

to believe that such crude representations could have been executed for any religious or civic purpose.

There has been considerable speculation about the purpose of the rectangular groove on the top surface of the Stone of Destiny. The only credible, though unlikely, hypothesis is that it was cut to hold a plaque. Indeed Edward I did cause such a tablet to be inscribed with a poem in mediaeval Latin, and it was hung adjacent to the Coronation Chair, although there is no claim that it was ever intended to be fixed to the stone itself. The following contemporary translation captures the vainglorious thoughts of Edward who compared himself to mythical Greek and Roman heroes.

> If the old chronicles have real truth
> Here, enclosed in this throne, is the famous Stone.
> On which the excellent Jacob, the former Patriarch,
> put his head when he saw the angels.
> Edward the First, our most powerful Hector
> conqueror of the Scots, took it from the Scots,
> As a just victor like a valiant Mars.
> To the glory of the English, and military renown.[2]

The end faces of the Stone of Destiny have had iron staples inserted using lead, and to these are fixed figure of eight links which are attached to iron rings. The purpose of the links and rings is evidently to enable the stone to be lifted. Grooves have been cut in the ends of the stone so that the links do not protrude beyond the face. Nonetheless, the staples did protrude and these have been filed down. It has been suggested that when the measurements specifying the dimensions of the Stone of Destiny were given to Master Walter, the carpenter, who, on Edward I's instructions, constructed the throne, they did not allow for the projections of the staples, and the Stone was therefore too big to fit into the throne. And so after the Stone of Destiny arrived in London, the ends of the

---

2 In Edward I's time most educated people would have understood these classical references. In Greek mythology, Hector was a Trojan prince and the greatest warrior of Troy during the Trojan war. In Roman mythology, Mars was the god of war, who through his affair with Venus, the god of love, fathered the Trojan hero, Aeneas, who was the founder of the city of Rome. Aeneas was the grandfather of Brutus who, legends assert, conquered Albion (England, Scotland and Wales) naming it Britain after himself, and became its first king. Brutus was considered to be the ancestor of all English kings. See Chapter 2.

staples had to be filed down to enable the Stone to be slid into its housing under the seat of the throne.

The end face of the Stone of Destiny showing the figure of eight link and the ring countersunk into the top surface.

The front, back and bottom faces of the Stone of Destiny have been dressed, but not to the same standard as the top, and the corners at the bottom have broken away. A view of the 'back' face of the Stone of Destiny reveals a vertical line, which is the cement-filled crack where the Stone of Destiny was broken during the raid on the Abbey in 1950.

When the Stone of Destiny was being prepared by Historic Environment Scotland for its journey to London for the coronation of Charles III, the opportunity was taken to study it again using the most modern digital technology. Thousands of photographs, taken with a DSLR camera, have enabled a 3D-printed replica to be created, allowing a more detailed study of the different tool marks made by the various craftsmen who fashioned the Stone. Remarkably, it has also revealed a line of four small, previously unrecorded, marks along the rough edge between the front and bottom surfaces of the stone. These marks are faint, and quite small, being about 10 mm in size, and have the appearance of the Roman numerals X, X, X, and V. No one has speculated about the significance or provenance of these markings.

X-ray fluorescence analysis was also undertaken to determine the elemental composition of the Stone. This confirmed its source from the quarries at Kincarrathie. It also led to the discovery of traces of a copper alloy on the upper surface which coincides with the dark stain near the centre of the top surface. This suggests that a copper, bronze or brass object was in contact with the Stone for a considerable time during its history. Once again no one has suggested an explanation for this stain.

Chapter 2
Early Myths and Legends

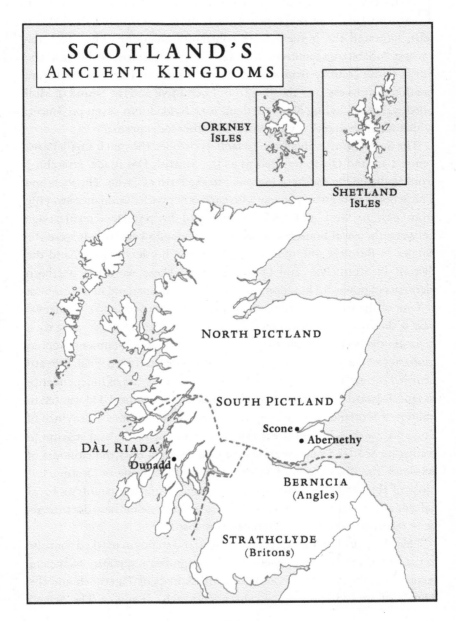

SCOTLAND'S
ANCIENT KINGDOMS

ORKNEY
ISLES

SHETLAND
ISLES

NORTH PICTLAND

SOUTH PICTLAND

Scone

Abernethy

DÀL RIADA

Dunadd

BERNICIA
(Angles)

STRATHCLYDE
(Britons)

The Scots: A Middle Eastern Celtic Tribe on the Move

FOLLOWING THE WITHDRAWAL of the Romans from Scotland in the second century, the country was roughly divided into four, although the borders were constantly changing. The Picts, the earliest inhabitants, controlled by far the greatest area – the east and north of the country from the modern counties of Fife and Perthshire north to Caithness, and the area from Loch Etive and the Sound of Mull northwards, including Skye. Pictland was divided into seven provinces, which were constantly vying with each other for supremacy.

The Scots, immigrants from Ireland, controlled the much smaller area centred around Oban, referred to as the Scottish Dàl Riada, stretching from Mull and the southern Hebrides to the Firth of Clyde. The Picts and The Scots were regularly at war with each other with dominance swaying from east to west and back, complicated by regular intermarriage between the royal households. South of Scotland's central belt were the Angles in Bernicia, the modern Lothian and Borders regions, and the Britons in Strathclyde and Dumfries-shire. These were the northern elements of powerful kingdoms based in Northumberland and Cumbria.

One of the major problems for researchers into Scotland's mediaeval past is the lack of historical records. It is not that there never were such records, it is because many of the official records and documents kept in monasteries and other institutions were stolen or destroyed when Edward I surged through Scotland at the beginning of the Wars of Independence in 1296. Edward's objective was cultural as well as political. He wanted to obliterate Scotland as a sovereign state, and establish it as a province of England, much as he had already done in Wales. And so, in an attempt to confiscate Scotland's national memory, he took not only the Honours of Scotland, the Black Rood of St Margaret, and the Stone of Destiny, but most of the official records and manuscripts from the country's royal palaces and monasteries and much else as well. Some of these documents were returned in the 1930s, but most were lost.

This absence of medieval records in Scotland stands in marked contrast to the situation in Ireland, where there is a significant quantity of ancient records, notably the Annals of Ulster, the Annals of Tigernach and the Annals of Innisfallen and the 'Duan Albanach' ('Song of The Scots') which is an Irish poetical record dating from the eleventh century. These Irish records provide much of the scant information that there is about the kings of the Scottish Dàl Riada and those of the Picts. This surviving information is mostly confined to lists of kings, how long they reigned, some of their relationships, and occasionally the manner of their death. The lists illustrate the changing fortunes of the Picts and The Scots due to wars and intermarriage. For example, during the period from 736 to 750, no kings of the Scottish Dàl Riada are detailed and, consequently, it appears that Dàl Riada was under the control of the Picts, or perhaps ruled by subordinate kings. The triumph of King Kenneth MacAlpin over the Picts in 843 was the last of a series of changing fortunes which had persisted probably for over 300 years.

Information regarding the ancestry of The Scots and the origin of the Stone of Destiny, comes from both Irish and Scottish sources, and comprises historical fact, legend and myth. The various sources give different accounts, occasionally more than one in a single narrative. They are frequently contradictory, with gaps and impossible timescales for a single lifespan, and sometimes they are clearly fantastical. Nevertheless, there are some threads running through them which demonstrate a very strong and unifying cultural memory.

The earliest written account of Scotland's early history is Baldred Bisset's *Processus* of 1301. Bisset was a senior clergyman in St Andrews Cathedral and became a professor of Canon Law at the University of Bologna. During the interregnum following the abdication of King John Balliol, Bisset was one of three Scots who were sent to Rome to present to the Papal Curia, the Court of Pope Boniface VIII, the case against Edward I's claims of suzerainty over Scotland. Edward's case for overlordship (also presented to the Pope) was based on the legend that Brutus, the Brute of Troy, who was descended from the Trojan hero Anaeas, conquered Albion (England, Scotland and Wales), and renamed it Britain after himself. On his death, Britain was divided up, and his eldest son, Locrinus, became King of England, his second son, Albanactus, became King of Scotland, and his third son, Kamber, took Wales. The descendants of Albanactus and Kamber, being the younger sons, were therefore subordinate to the descendants of Locrinus.

Bisset's objective was to show that the kings of Scots were not descended from Brutus but came from a Middle Eastern tribe which had left Palestine following the Biblical Exodus and made their way over many centuries via the Mediterranean, Spain, and after a sojourn in Ireland, to Argyll. Bisset emphasised The Scots connection with the Biblical Middle East, as being among God's chosen peoples, and he cunningly exploited Edward's seizure of the Stone of Destiny, and its installation in Westminster as evidence that Edward recognised the antiquity of Scotland's development, and that it was different from England's. The crucial date for establishing Scotland's right to an independent existence (that is, independent from England) was the year 500, and the inauguration on the Stone of Destiny of Fergus Mòr mac Eric, who is acknowledged to be the first king of Scots.

Perhaps the most important account of the origin of The Scots, despite its brevity, was the Declaration of Arbroath, written in 1320, and based on Bisset's *Processus*, although it does not mention the Stone of Destiny. This was a letter from the clergy and nobles of Scotland to the Pope seeking his support in the continuing standoff with the Crown in London. The account of the wanderings of The Scots considered the forerunners of the Scottish nation are referred to in the preamble to the Declaration, where it states that the starting point of their migration was Scythia. This is the area to the north of the Black Sea, which includes modern Crimea, Ukraine and Romania:

> Most Holy Father, we know, and from the chronicles and books of the ancients we find that among other famous nations our own, the Scots, has been graced with widespread renown. They journeyed from Greater Scythia by way of the Tyrrhenian Sea (off the west coast of modern Italy) and the Pillars of Hercules (Straits of Gibraltar), and dwelt for a long course of time in Spain among the most savage peoples but nowhere could it be subdued by any people, however barbarous. Thence it came, twelve hundred years after the people of Israel crossed the Red Sea, to its home in the west where it still lives today.

At that time, and indeed up to the present day, many nations have sought to claim to be among 'God's chosen people'. This claim is stated unambiguously in the Declaration of Arbroath, in a paragraph which immediately follows the previous quotation:

> The high qualities and merits of these people, were they not otherwise manifest, shine forth clearly enough from this: that the King of kings and Lord of lords, our Lord Jesus Christ, after His Passion and Resurrection, called them, even though settled in the uttermost parts of the earth, almost the first to His most holy faith. Nor did He wish them to be confirmed in that faith by merely anyone but by the first of His Apostles – by calling, though second or third in rank – the most gentle Saint Andrew, the Blessed Peter's brother, and desired him to keep them under his protection as their patron for ever.

The references to St Andrew and Scythia are related. Bernard de Linton, the Abbot of Arbroath, who was the main author of the Declaration would have known that the Pope would be well aware that St Andrew, following the crucifixion of Jesus, travelled north to evangelise the peoples around the Bosporus and the Black Sea, and hence he became the patron saint of Russia and Romania, and also, of course, of Scotland.

The claim to be among God's chosen peoples was bolstered by the legend that the Stone of Destiny was the pillow used by Jacob, as described in Chapter 28 of the Book of Genesis in the Old Testament of the Bible. According to this Biblical story, Jacob was the son of Isaac and grandson of Abraham, who could claim descent from Noah (of the Ark) and indeed from Adam and Eve in the Garden of Eden. Both Abraham and Isaac had been promised by God that they would be the founding fathers of a great nation which God would protect and nurture. This nation would be in effect, 'God's chosen people'. However, Abraham had only one legitimate son (Isaac), and Isaac had two (twins, Jacob and Esau), and so it was not until the third generation that God's promise to Abraham, reiterated to Isaac and in due course to Jacob, began to be fulfilled.

The account in the Book of Genesis states that Jacob was on a journey with his entourage to visit his father-in-law's extended family in order to find a suitable wife. At nightfall, he made a bed of stones on which to sleep, and during the night he had a dream in which he saw a vision of a ladder connecting heaven and earth, with the 'the angels of God ascending and descending upon it' (Genesis 28:12). He then heard the voice of God promising (as it had done to his father and grandfather before him) 'that thy seed shall be as the dust of the earth, and that thou shalt spread abroad to the west, and the east and to the north and the south' (Genesis 28:14). When he woke up – the Bible chronicles – Jacob used the stone that had been under his head and set it up as a pillar (Genesis 28:18) and poured oil upon it. In due course, he fathered twelve sons who became the heads of the twelve tribes of Israel.[1]

There is no record whatsoever in the Biblical story that Jacob retained one of the stones for any other purpose, and the myth that his pillow became the Stone of Destiny was probably added to the story by monks in the tenth century, to emphasise the concept that The Scots were among 'God's chosen peoples'.

The claim in the Declaration that The Scots were 'special' in God's sight chimes with the claims of many nationalities, including the English. Scotland was no different from many other peoples across the world which have sought to justify such a claim, usually by attempting to assert descent from one of the twelve tribes of Israel. Colquhoun, for example, claims in the preface to his book, *Our Descent from Israel* (published in Glasgow in 1931, with a second edition in 1949), that there is:

> a vast amount of evidence, proving beyond question that the Anglo-Saxon-Celtic peoples of the British Empire...are the literal ethnical descendants of the House of Israel and the Hebrew migrants from Egypt and Canaan.

The evidence quoted by Colquhoun, although voluminous, is, as he admits, entirely circumstantial, and does not bear rigorous examination. Furthermore, Colquhoun quotes no scientific data to back it up.

With the exception of Bisset's *Processus*, the historical chronicles of Scotland's past are accounts written after the conclusion of the Wars of Independence with the Treaty of Edinburgh-Northampton in 1328. Nevertheless, it is known that these chroniclers relied on sources, since lost, dating from around a century or more earlier and certainly on oral

---

1 The word 'pillow' features in the King James Version of the Bible, but not in more modern translations.

traditions. It is important to realise therefore, that the legends, particularly regarding the origin of the Stone of Destiny were well established long before the theft of the Stone in 1296, and were not, as some have suggested, an attempt to mythologise the Stone after it had been lost.

Important among these records are:

John of Fordun's *Chronicle of the Scottish People*, which was probably written in 1371, some 75 years after Edward's raid.

Walter Bower's *Scotichronicon* dating from around 1440; *Scalacronica* written between 1355 and 1363, by Sir Thomas Grey of Heaton in Northumbria.

Andrew of Wyntoun's *The Orygynale Cronykil* (Original Chronicle') – written in about 1440 at St Serf's Priory on St Serfs Inch, an island in Loch Leven in Kinross-shire.

Much later, in 1527, Hector Boece, an historian educated in Dundee and Paris, who became the first principal of Aberdeen University, combined the various legends in his *Scotorum historiae*, which covered Scottish history from 330 BC to 1437. It was dedicated to James V, and for many centuries was accepted as the definitive history of Scotland. Because James V could not read Latin, John Bellenden (or Ballantyne) translated the original into Scots in 1536, as his *Croniklis of Scotland*. This was a very free, accessible translation and it ensured that Boece's account achieved a wide circulation. It was not just a translation for it contained details not in the original. A verse edition in Scots, *Buik of the Croniclis of Scotland*, was also produced for James V, by the courtier, William Stewart, and presented to the monarch in 1535, although it was not published until more than 300 years later in 1858. It too is a very free translation and has information not in either of the earlier works.

The Stone of Destiny is also referred to in a number of English accounts, including William of Rishanger's *Chronica et Annales*, dating from about 1327.

★ ★ ★

The Exodus from Egypt and Arrival in Ireland

At least the story of Jacob's Pillow, although fantastical, is universal throughout the various sources in which it is mentioned. Further episodes in the accounts of the origin of the Stone of Destiny and The Scots people vary considerably, but the fundamentals of the story are fairly consistent. The most important legends are those referring to Scota, the daughter of a Pharaoh, who was the founding matriarch, and who gave her name to The Scots. In some accounts, however, there are two personalities named Scota, separated by many generations. Then there is the husband of Scota, Gaythelos (or Gaidelon), perhaps a Scythian or Greek nobleman, whose name is said to be the origin of the word Gael and even, according to some more far-fetched accounts, of Galloway.

The main characters in these stories are Moses, Scota and Gaythelos. Also important are a serpent and a prophesy which is central to understanding how this wandering Celtic tribe understood its destiny. The journey they took from the Middle East via the shores of the Mediterranean Sea, to North Africa, Spain and Ireland is reiterated in some form or other in all the accounts, although sometimes with elements of the tale omitted.

John of Fordun's *Chronicle of the Scottish People*, which is basically a compilation of early myths and legends, but with details from other sources, claims that in the period before the Biblical Exodus from Egypt, a Greek nobleman, Gaythelos, a contemporary of Moses, was a guest of the Pharaoh. He was married to Scota, the daughter of the Pharaoh. One day, when he was with Moses, he was bitten by a venomous snake. However, he was cured by Moses who went on to promise that no serpent or other poisonous creature would inhabit the western island that the descendants of Gaythelos would rule over one day.

Moses is also said to have given the Stone of Destiny to Scota, as recorded in the song 'La Pierre d'Écosse':[2]

> In Egypt, Moses preached to the people.
> Scota, Pharaoh's daughter, listened well,
> For he said to the spirit, 'Whoso will possess this stone,
> Shall be the conqueror of a very far off land.

---

2 'La Pierre d'Écosse' is a song composed in 1307 and is the earliest English reference to the Stone of Destiny.

Unlike the stories about Jacob's Pillow, the prophesies relating to Moses, and the legends about Scota and Gaythelos do not feature in the Bible.

According to the Bible, Moses later became the leader of the Israelites during their rebellion against the oppressive conditions of their slavery in Egypt and became God's instrument in bringing about the plagues which devastated the Egyptians, and eventually persuaded the Pharaoh to expel the Israelites. The Israelites left *en mass* heading for Sinai on the other side of the Red Sea. However, after they had left, the Pharaoh changed his mind and pursued them to the coast. Under God's command, Moses caused the waters of the Red Sea to part and allow the Israelites to cross to the other side, but then released the waters which engulfed the pursuing Egyptians.

According to the legends, Gaythelos, on account of his friendship with Moses, had refused to assist his host, the Pharaoh, in his persecution and pursuit of the Israelites, and so was banished from Egypt. And that is why he, Scota and their tribe left Egypt with, so it is said, the Stone of Destiny.

In a slightly different version of the story, Gaythelos was just a young man when he met Moses, and was bitten by the snake, and it was his grandson, Niul, who was the guest of the Pharaoh, married Scota and was expelled from Egypt.

Another version claims that the people of Israel kept the sacred pillow stone that Jacob had used on that fateful night, and eventually it found its way into the Temple of Jerusalem. When that was about to be ransacked by the Babylonians, it was taken to Egypt, where it became known as the Pharaoh's Stone. At this junction the two legends unite, for the Pharaoh's Stone becomes the property of one of the Pharaoh's daughters, Scota, who having been driven out of Egypt leads her migrant tribe around the Mediterranean, and eventually comes to Spain.

Sojourn in Spain

As the legends describe, after Scota and her husband were driven out of Egypt with their families, they wandered around the Mediterranean, and eventually settled in the northwest corner of Spain, which is now the Spanish province of Galicia, where they built the town of Brigancia.[3]

---

3 Brigancia became the Roman town of Brigantium and is now Corunna.

This journey from the Middle East to Spain was not a stampede or a forced march, but a very gradual migration, which probably took at least a thousand years. It is during their time in Galicia that the legends first refer to a sacred stone which was used by The Scots in Spain on royal occasions and as a seat of justice.

According to some versions of the tradition, all of this took place during the lifetime of Gaythelos. Just before Gaythelos died, according to these accounts, his family, now identified as The Scots in Spain, were being harassed by the hostile natives, and so Gaythelos sent an expedition to seek out a new territory across the sea. It is said that he built a tower and, from its top it is said that he could see Ireland on the horizon (notwithstanding the fact that it is over 500 miles away across the Atlantic).[4] The expedition was successful, and Ireland was invaded by Scota and her two sons, Hyber (from which the name Hibernia is derived) and Hymer.

Celtic Culture in Galicia

Classical authors, writing during the first century, describe a Celtic tribe which inhabited the northwest of Spain, which was clearly different from the other neighbouring inhabitants. In particular, the tribe is understood to have had a different culture and spoke a unique language. The Roman author, Pliny the Elder, and the Roman mathematician, Ptolemy both refer to this Celtic tribe.

The name of the area, Galicia, is derived from *Gallaecia* which was the name of a Roman province in the northeast of Spain, covering approximately the same territory as the present day Galicia. The people of Galicia have maintained a distinctive culture, language and government since that time, and in 1981 it was protected by the Statute of Autonomy, which grants Galicia a devolved parliament and self-government comparable to the devolution enjoyed by Catalonia and the Basque region.

The fact is that the Galician people had managed to develop a culture distinct from other neighbouring tribes emanating from the same Asian source and inhabiting the same area. They were able to maintain that distinction for over 1,000 years prior to the invasion of Ireland, and indeed

---

4 This probably refers to the Tower of Hercules, a Roman lighthouse about 1.5 miles from Corunna. which was built in the first century, several centuries after the invasion of Ireland.

have retained and developed it right up to the present. In recent years, that has been manifest in the enthusiastic participation in traditional music and sport, and in renewed academic interest in their history and traditions.

Although the first century Galicians spoke a Celtic language, by the Middle Ages it had been superseded by a language related to Portuguese. By that time, however, they had developed their own music, dance, art and sport, which in many cases are similar to the equivalents found in Ireland, Highland Scotland and Brittany. In particular, the harp is said to have been brought from Galicia to Ireland, and later imported to Scotland where it is known as the clarsach. And bagpipes are still a popular traditional instrument in Galicia as in Ireland and Scotland. In the last few decades, the Galicians have been rediscovering their Celtic heritage, and developing cultural links with the other Celtic communities in the British Isles and Brittany. Lately, these cultural links have been reinforced by international festivals which mix participants, collaborators and audiences from all of the modern Celtic nations.

The Stone Comes to Ireland:
King Milo and Simon Brecc

John of Fordun's chronicle gives two quite incompatible accounts of the coming of the Stone of Destiny to Ireland from Spain. According to Fordun, by this time, probably about 500 BC, The Scots in Spain had built a significant colony in Galicia, centred around the site of the modern city of Corunna, with an established monarchy ('The Kings of The Scots in Spain'). They were, however, regularly harassed by local hostile tribes and, mindful of the prophesy of Moses that they would inhabit an island in the west where there were no venomous snakes, they looked across the Atlantic to Ireland.

The more detailed of John of Fordun's versions, elaborated in Wyntoun's chronicle, begins at the time that the legendary King of The Scots in Spain, King Milo, was on the throne. By this point, The Scots in Spain already had a ceremonial stone, used as a seat for the king on judicial occasions and at his inauguration. Fordun notes, fairly briefly, that this stone along with other regalia, had been brought to Spain from Egypt by Gaythelos (although there is no claim that it was Jacob's Pillow). Milo had three sons, but he favoured the youngest, Simon Brecc, who could not be his heir, and so he sent him with a fleet of ships and an army to invade and colonise Ireland. As he set sail, his father, as John of Fordun relates:

> presented him with a marble throne of very ancient workman-
> ship, carved by careful craftsmen on which the kings of the
> Scottish people (in Spain) used to sit.

The Irish legends report that:

> Milo prophesied to his son, who on being strengthened
> when he received the Stone, began to rejoice
> that his descendants would reign wherever he placed it.

John of Fordun also has King Milo echo Moses' prophesy, that wherever the stone should rest, there The Scots would reign:

> *Ni fallat fatum, Scoti quoncunque locatum,*
> *Invenient lapidem, Regnare tenatur ibidem*

This Latin couplet is best translated by Sir Walter Scott in his book, *History of Scotland*:

> Unless the fates are faithless found,
> And prophets' voice be vain,
> Where'er this monument be found.
> The Scottish race shall reign.

In due course, John of Fordun tells us, Simon Brecc conquered Ireland, set up the Stone of Destiny as his throne on the Hill of Tara and reigned there for many years.

John of Fordun's chronicle has a second very different account of the origin of the Stone of Destiny, but no explanation of the discrepancy between the two is given. In this second account, Simon Brecc after he reached Ireland, anchored off the coast. However, a storm intervened, and he attempted to raise his anchors to seek a better shelter. The story records that he did this with great difficulty, and that, 'along with his anchors he pulled into the ship a block of marble, cut in the shape of a throne'.

Remarkably, in Fordun's chronicle, there is no comment on the differences between the two accounts. It is also surprising that neither Fordun, nor any of the other chroniclers remark on the difference between the stone brought from Ireland for Fergus Mòr mac Eric's inauguration (marble with carvings by careful craftsmen), and the stone uplifted for Edward I (roughly-hewn sandstone). Perhaps none of the chroniclers, all of whom were writing decades after the event, were aware that Edward's stone was not marble, and did not have any carvings on it.

There are various versions of these legends, with different names for the personalities involved and different timescales. They each emphasise different elements of the story, depending at least in part on their origin – whether Irish or Scottish. For example, some of the Irish legends talk about three separate invasions of Ireland from Galicia, and others refer to six. Whatever is the truth about the stories of 'invasions' in primitive ships across over 500 miles of the Atlantic Ocean, what is most likely is that there was a steady drift of people from Galicia to Ireland, stimulated by trade, but punctuated by more violent episodes.

In a different account which omits all references to Scythia, North Africa and Spain, Scota, carrying with her the 'royal seat', is said to have sailed from Egypt with a large fleet, and landed in Ireland. There she took aboard some Irishmen, and sailed on to Scotland, where she overthrew the Picts, and established her kingdom. It is notable, also, that the account in the Declaration of Arbroath omits any specific mention of Ireland, stating only that The Scots travelled from greater Scythia via the Tyrrhenian Sea, the Pillars of Hercules and Spain, 'to its home in the west where it still lives today'.

Irish Legends

The origin stories of the Celtic peoples of Ireland and those of Scotland are clearly closely linked, and Ireland too has a sacred stone, the Lia Fàil. As with the Scottish legends, there are conflicting accounts of the origin of the Irish people in Ireland, and the source of its sacred stone. The legends in the Lebor Gabala or Book of Invasions (believed, until the middle of the nineteenth century to be the genuine factual history of Ireland) tells of six separate invasions of Ireland. During the fifth of these, the people known as the Tuatha Dè Danaan (People of the Goddess

Danu) were said to have brought the Lia Fàil to Ireland from the city of Falias in Greece and set it up at the Hill of Tara. The sixth and last invasion recorded in the *Lebor Gabala*, was by the Sons of Mill (perhaps the same as King Milo although Simon Brecc's name is not mentioned). The legend states that during this sixth invasion, the Lia Fàil was brought to Ireland from Spain, rather than from Greece.

According to another version of the Gaelic legends surrounding the Lia Fàil, a legend more associated with the Stone of Destiny, the sacred stone arrived by a ship belonging to the Iberian Danaan into the ancient port of Carrickfergus about 580 BC. On board was Eochaidh, son of a High King, Princess Tea Tephi, Scota and the scribe, Simon Brauch, and they delivered the stone to the Hill of Tara. Eochaidh is said to have taken the ancient stone from the temple in Jerusalem to save it from the invading Babylonians. Scota and Eochaidh had previously met in Jerusalem, and in due course they were married. The legends claim that all later Irish High Kings and British monarchs inaugurated on the Stone of Destiny can demonstrate lineage back to Eochaidh and his wife, Scota, the original bearers of the Stone from Egypt to Ireland.

There is no doubt that a strong folk-memory of a royal stone has existed in Ireland for many centuries. It was focused on the Hill of Tara, where the Lia Fàil can still be seen and where Simon Brecc is said to have placed the stone he brought from Galicia and set up his kingdom. While there is much confusion between Ireland's Lia Fàil and the Stone of Destiny, the Lia Fàil is an upright, 'standing stone', and although it was probably involved in Ireland's prehistoric royal rituals, it is not shaped like a seat or throne.

Prehistoric Origins of The Scots

The links between the Celtic Irish and Scottish people and the inhabitants of Galicia in Spain, as outlined in the ancient Scottish and Irish chronicles, is confirmed culturally as noted above. Nonetheless, the possibility that their Galician forebears may have originated in Scythia, as claimed in the Decoration of Arbroath, is now suggested, by some scholars, using the results of modern archaeology and the widespread genetic testing of modern European populations.

During the Bronze Age, the Yamnaya peoples of the Steppes (modern

Ukraine, Bulgaria, Romania and eastern Russia) began a slow, but inexorable, migration to the west, a process which took perhaps 2,000 years. The Scythians were renowned for their horsemanship and mastery of the bow and arrow, which gave them military superiority over the people they displaced as they moved westwards. They developed their culture as they went to become the Bell Beaker Folk, so described from the characteristic shapes of the bell-shaped beakers found among their grave goods.

It is argued that at least 90 per cent of modern Scots and Irish people, and a large proportion of French, Spanish and other European peoples are descendants of these early migrants. A map of the spread of the Yamnaya, which is said to have been the largest migration in European history, shows how they moved gradually, over many hundreds of years, from Scythia (north of the Black Sea) into Western Europe extending through Italy and France, and reaching as far north as Norway and also spreading along the coast of North Africa, and across the Straits of Gibraltar into Spain.[5] This latter route is exactly the journey described in the Declaration of Arbroath. Within the generality of the Bell Beaker Folk DNA, more recent DNA markers can be detected. Perhaps least surprising is the concentration of particular DNA markers in the west of Scotland, particularly Argyll, and in the north-east of Ireland – the old kingdom of Dàl Riada.

The fact that The Scots were descended from the same prehistoric ancestors from the Steppes, as neighbouring tribes and peoples who also inhabited the land around Galicia, does not negate the fact that they were different – culturally distinct if not genetically unique. The area of Scythia is enormous – much bigger than France – and there would have been many different tribes, and languages within it. Furthermore, different tribes would have embarked on their migration at different times, during the 2,000 years that it took place, so it is not surprising that a variety of cultures persisted.

Particularly interesting are recent linguistic studies, noted by Alistair Moffat and Jim Wilson in their book, *The Scots. A Genetic Journey*, which have shown unexpected similarities between Scots and Irish Gaelic andsome of the languages spoken along the coast of North Africa.[6]

---

5 I am greatly indebted to Jim Wilson, Professor of Human Genetics at Edinburgh University, for the information about the Yamnaya people and the Bell Beaker folk.

6 Alastair Moffat and James F Wilson, *The Scots. A Genetic Journey* (Edinburgh: Birlinn, 2011).

Gaelic has a number of unique ways of saying things which are not shared by any other European language apart from some North African languages, in particular Berber, Egyptian Arabic and Maltese, and also, interestingly, Russian. For example, Gaelic does not have a word for the verb, 'to have'. Instead Gaelic uses a combination of the verb 'to be' and the various elements of the prepositional pronoun derived from the preposition 'aig' meaning 'at'. In order to say, 'I have a coat', a Scottish Gaelic speaker will say, 'Tha cota agam', which is translated literally is, 'A coat is at me'. Agam is a combination of the preposition 'aig' (at) and the pronoun 'mi' (me). Another example is the sentence, 'Mary is a teacher'. In Scottish Gaelic, it is "S e tidsear a th' ann an Màiri'. This is translated literally as, 'It is a teacher that is in Mary'.

The existence of these and several other locutions shared with the ancient North African languages is a pointer to a common heritage going back three millennia, and is consistent with modern archaeological and DNA evidence.

Timescales

The relationship between the archaeological, linguistic and scientific data about migration of The Scots, and the cultural memory of it, as related in the various chronicles, is important when attempting to assess the historical veracity of the events recorded in these accounts. The migration may have taken 1,000 years to progress from the Black Sea coast to Spain, a further thousand years to consolidate its position in Spain before crossing to Ireland in around 500 BC, and yet another 1,000 years before The Scots from the Irish Dàl Riada secured their base in Argyll in Scotland. And so the chronicles available to us today, which were compiled between 800 and 1,000 years after that final move, and long before any scientific studies were available, must rely almost entirely on oral legends and cultural memory, with all the potential bias and inaccuracies which that involves. And yet, as we have seen, the limited scientific evidence that has emerged tends to support the basic elements of the narrative, and does not contradict it.

Chapter 3
The Stone of Destiny Comes to Scotland and to Scone

Origin of Dàl Riada

BY THE FOURTH CENTURY, The Scots had thoroughly colonised the island of Ireland, and over time a hierarchical system of kings had developed. Historically there were five provinces, each of which was ruled by an overking, who was subject to the High King of All Ireland who ruled from the Hill of Tara, where the Stone of Destiny was located. The boundaries of these provinces, however, were moveable, and frequently over the centuries there were more than five provinces. These provinces were divided into smaller territories or subkingdoms, each of which was ruled by a king who was subject to the king of his province. In some cases, there were further subdivisions and tiers of kingly authority.

The territory of the subkingdom of Dàl Riada was a part of what is now Ulster, and consisted of the strip of land along the northeast coast between Lough Foyle and Belfast Lough, with its power base at Dunseverick Castle, near the Giant's Causeway. The kingdom had been established, or perhaps consolidated, by Cairbre Riada, an Irish nobleman of high descent, between 254 and 273. Riada was his name, and 'Cairbre' means 'long arm' – 'Riada with the long arms'. 'Dàil'.[1] is the old Irish Gaelic word for 'portion', or 'share', usually of land, and was generally followed by the name of the owner or ruler of that land. In due course, it came to mean the territory of the descendants of that ruler. Dàl Riada therefore was the historic territory of Cairbre Riada's clan.

While travel overland through the Antrim Hills to other parts of Ireland was difficult, slow and hazardous, sailing across the narrow North Channel between Dàl Riada and Argyll and the islands of Scotland was easily accomplished by experienced sailors. And so, during the first half of the first millennium AD, much of Argyll and the Inner Hebrides had been settled by Scots immigrants from the northeast of Ireland and had become part of the Irish subkingdom of Dàl Riada.

1 In modern Scottish Gaelic, it is spelled 'Dàil'.

Fergus Son of Ferchard and Fergus Mòr mac Eric

The history of this period is confusing not least because there were two kings named 'Fergus', both of whom were the 'first' of their line, although separated by several hundred years. Also both were said to have been inaugurated on the Stone of Destiny. A major difficulty for historians is that the accounts of the events, as recorded in the various chronicles by Fordun, Boece, Buchanan, Monipennie and others, were all written more than 1,000 years after the events they purport to record, and some of the sources that they used have since been shown to be erroneous, so it is small wonder that there are discrepancies and contradictions. Nevertheless, the chronicles do make it possible to deduce a plausible, if very speculative, calendar of events, covering the period from the immigration of The Scots into Argyll until the inauguration of Fergus Mòr mac Eric in 500.

The immigrant Argyllshire Scots set up, in due course, their own subkingdom, which was subservient to the kings of the Irish Dàl Riada. According to Boece, the first king of the Argyllshire Dàl Riada was Fergus, son of Ferchard, an Irish prince, who defeated the Picts and established himself as the first of a line of 'Forty Kings' who ruled in Argyll in the early part of the first millennium. It is said that he brought the 'Chair' from Ireland to Argyll and was crowned on it. While some historians consider that the 'Forty Kings' are all mythical, one of them at least, Ewen, said to be the twelfth king after Fergus son of Ferchard, left a heritage which, we shall see, is not so easily dismissed.

In 1869, William F Skene, the doyen of Victorian Scottish antiquarians, examined the existing evidence at that time and claimed that Fergus, son of Ferchard, built a principal town called Beregonium probably on the north side of Loch Etive, perhaps near the site of Oban Airport, or a little further north near the modern village of Benderloch.[2] This may have been destroyed by fire, but in any case it was succeeded by a new town built by King Ewen, and called after him Evonium. It was built 'not far away' from Beregonium, perhaps on the flat land adjacent to the site of Dunstaffnage Castle, on the other side of Loch Etive. This account is confirmed by William Stewart in his metrical translation of Boece's *Scotorum Historiae*, in which he records that Ewen built a castle on the

---

2 William F Skene, *The Coronation Stone* (Edinburgh: Edmonston & Douglas, 1869).

Dunstaffnage site and called it *Dun Euone* after his name. Ewen, however, was not the first to occupy the site, for there is evidence of a pre-existing Stone-Age fort on the rock.

Beregonium, Evonium, Dun Monaidh and Dunstaffnage

Dunstaffnage Castle features strongly in folk memory and in many of the ancient chronicles and also in modern photographs and postcards, and yet the castle which we see today was not built until long after the events associated with The Scots and the Stone of Destiny took place. The name Dunstaffnage is a mixture of Gaelic and Norse. 'Dun', is of course, the Gaelic word for 'a fort'. 'Staffnage' is a minor corruption of the compound Norse word 'staff-ness' – 'staff' meaning 'a stick of wood', and 'ness' meaning 'a promontory' – 'the Fort on the Wooded Promontory'. As a name with even a partial Norse origin, it could not have been in use before the ninth century. Prior to that it was called Dun Monaidh – a Gaelic name which may be related linguistically to Evonium. Confusingly, the historians of this period tend to move seamlessly between Beregonium, Evonium, Dun Monaidh and Dunstaffnage.

The existing stone castle was built early in the thirteenth century, probably around 1220. It is a formidable and eminently defendable structure,

Dunstaffnage Castle, overlooking Dunstaffnage Bay.

perched on a rocky outcrop that pierces the grassy bank around it, with the main entrance up a long staircase overlooked by a high wall.

King Ewen's castle would have been built of wood and was almost certainly modified and strengthened by subsequent kings. It is said that it was the base for the Gaelic kings of the Scottish Dàl Riada for several centuries, and its situation emphasises why that was the case. It is perched on top of a volcanic plug of rock and is surrounded on three sides by the sea. It overlooks a sheltered bay with a pebble beach which provided a secure anchorage and was ideal for hauling up the birlinns of the occupying force. At a time when the highways of Scotland were its long sea lochs and narrow sounds, there can be no doubt about the strategic importance of the site of Dunstaffnage. The castle looks west across the Firth of Lorne to the Sound of Mull which provided access for the sea-going birlinns of the kings of Dàl Riada to Skye and the northwest coast of Scotland and to Ireland. To the northeast, Loch Linnhe could take them to the Great Glen and the very heart of northern Scotland, and to the east was the route via Loch Etive to the Pass of Brander, and central Scotland. To the south, lay the Firth of Clyde, and the islands of Jura and Islay. The castle may well have been a location of the Stone of Destiny at various times in its history, although there is no supporting documentary evidence.

By the end of the fifth century, during the reign of the last of the 'Forty Kings', The Scots of Dàl Riada were overcome, probably by the Picts, and beaten back to Ireland. It may be that they took the Stone of Destiny back with them to Ireland because there are references to the Stone travelling 'to and fro' across the Irish Sea. But it was not to be for long, because another Fergus, Fergus Mòr mac Eric, nephew of the last of the 'Forty Kings', aided by forces from his relatives in Ireland, reconquered the Scottish Dàl Riada, probably in 498, and Fergus was installed as king, but subordinate to the king of the Irish Dàl Riada.

Fergus clearly valued the authority which a proper inauguration on the Stone of Destiny would confer. Boece recounts how the Stone was brought to Scotland from Tara in 500. The High King of Ireland, Murtagh mac Eric, loaned it to his relative, Fergus Mòr mac Eric, when Fergus became king, so that it could be used at his inauguration in Scotland.

We are not told where the inauguration of Fergus Mòr took place, but *Chronica Rhythmicum* states that it was in *Ergadia* (Argyll). It certainly

could not have been Iona because the inauguration happened long before
Columba arrived on the island in 563, and Iona, before Columba, was not
a sacred island. The inauguration was a major event celebrated by the
nobility from far and wide. It was planned that it should be remembered
by posterity by engraving the acclamation, 'Fergus and his succession in
heritage shall ever hold this crown', a version of King Milo's prophecy.
This was said to be engraved on the Stone of Destiny in letters of gold, as
recorded by William Stewart:

> And all the rest with one loud voice on high,
> 'Fergus', they said, 'and his succession
> in heritage shall ever hold this crown'.
> Then all were sworn to keep that loyal and true,
> For more effect, in great letters of Greek,
> engraved these words onto a large stone,
> well gilded with gold as it should never be gone.[3]

Folk memory confirms that Evonium/Dun Monaidh/Dunstaffnage
was the site of the inaugurations of the kings of Dàl Riada from the time
of Fergus Mòr, when the Stone of Destiny was brought to Scotland until
it was taken to Iona for King Aìdàn's inauguration by Columba in 574.
Indeed, it may have been the site of inaugurations of the rulers of the
Scottish Dàl Riada before Fergus Mòr. It was here too that the early kings
were buried. It was also, in due course, the site of a 'cell' or church
established by the Irish monk St Màol-Rubha.[4]

Presumably, since we are told that the Stone of Destiny was only
loaned to Fergus by Murtagh mac Eric, the High King of Ireland at Tara,
it should have been returned to Ireland. However, not long after the
inauguration, Fergus and his entourage were caught in a storm in Belfast
Lough and their birlinn foundered on a rock off Carrickfergus, and all
were drowned.[5] And so the Stone remained in Scotland, and Irish sources
acknowledge that Murtagh mac Eric was the last High King of Ireland to

---

3 *Buik of the Cronicils of Scotland*, William Stewart, c1535.

4 See the Knights Templar, Chapter 9.

5 'Carrick' is derived from the Gaelic word 'carraig' and the Old Welsh word 'carreg', both
meaning a 'rock'. Carrickfergus – the 'Rock of Fergus'.

be crowned on the Stone of Destiny.

Fergus Mòr established the Scottish royal dynasty and all Scottish monarchs up to James VI, were proud to claim their descent from him. Indeed, James wrote in a letter to his wife, Anne of Denmark, affirming that he, 'was a happie Monarch sprung of Fergus race'.

Iona, St Columba and the Stone of Destiny

The evidence that the Stone of Destiny was taken to Iona is meagre, but tantalising. It rests on two texts, and on our knowledge of the personality of St Columba.

The earliest Scottish mention of the Stone is in the Gaelic poem, composed probably in 1060, 'The Birth of Àedàn MacGabràin', (a grandson of Fergus Mòr) in which it is referred to as the 'Eastern Stone'. According to the poem, Àedàn was inaugurated as King of Scots on the Stone of Destiny on Iona by St Columba in 574. There is confirmation of that inauguration in the biography of St Columba written by St Cumine the White, the seventh Abbot of Iona, writing nearly 100 years after the event in 660, and also in the Life of St Columba written by St Adomnàn, the ninth Abbot, in about 700. 'This was the first record of the inauguration of a monarch to be sanctioned by the Pope, but it is worth noting that neither biographies mention the Stone of Destiny in their accounts of the event'.

The second text which states explicitly that the Stone of Destiny was taken to Iona is in Wyntoun's chronicle which relates that:

> ...Fergus Mòr mac Eric
> Brought this stone within Scotlande,
> First quhen he come and won that land
> and set if first in Icolmkyll.
> and Scone there eftyr was brought til.[6]

The timescales in the chronicle have obviously been telescoped for, as noted above, Fergus was drowned in 501 shortly after his inauguration, which was more than 60 years before Columba went to Iona. And so it is likely that it was Àidàn mac Gabràin who took the Stone to Iona for his own inauguration in 574.

One of the factors not often considered when discussing the provenance

6 Quhen – when; Icolmkyll – Iona; there eftyr – thereafter

of the Stone of Destiny is the origin, family history and character of Columba. He was one of the most important and influential figures of his age, and was very much involved in the governance of the Scottish Dàl Riada of Pictland, of the Irish Dàl Riada and indeed of Ireland generally.

He was born in 521 in Donegal of royal parentage, with an impressive list of antecedents. Among his great grandparents were Niall of the Nine Hostages, the first of the High Kings of Ireland, who ruled the country from Tara, and King Conall Gulban, the founder of the royal dynasty of Donegal. His first cousin was King Ainmire, the ruling High King at Tara at that time. His family also had links with the Uì Nèill, the noblest family in Ireland, and his mother came from the royal house of Leinster. In Ireland, kingship did not pass automatically by the law of primogeniture, but by election from among a small family group who were eligible for succession and had the 'material of kingship'.[7] Columba was very well-placed in that group, and if he had had kingly ambitions it is likely that he would have succeeded, perhaps even to become High King at Tara.

Columba was also a poet, and in his early twenties became a disciple of Gemman, the Bard of Leinster. He was steeped in the customs and traditions of Ireland and of the kings both of Ireland and of the Scottish Dàl Riada. He would certainly have been aware of the history and importance of the Stone of Destiny.

Notwithstanding the fact that he withdrew his candidature for the highest royal appointments in Ireland, he remained a very political person. While the establishing of Christ's kingdom across all of Scotland was his most important objective, he was also a skilled diplomat and he championed peace, reconciliation and, as we shall see, the continuity of tradition.

Iona was on the north-western extremity of Scottish Dàl Riada close to the disputed border with northern Pictland, the territory of King Brude, a powerful Pictish king of northern Scotland, whose stronghold was on Loch Ness, perhaps on the site of Castle Urquhart. The island of Iona was unoccupied (or at least unclaimed) when Columba arrived and it was granted to him by his cousin, Conall MacComgaill, the sixth king of Scottish Dàl Riada, after Fergus Mòr. After setting up his monastery,

---

7 This system was continued in Scotland and was in use until after the time of Macbeth.

Columba's first missionary journey was to visit King Brude in his northern stronghold. While the main objective of the journey was evangelical, to convert Brude and his people to Christianity (which he did), undoubtedly it was also diplomatic, to neutralise the threat from the Picts to the north of Mull. Wherever Columba went, he and his missionaries established 'cells' or churches – which he called significantly, 'sentries for Christ' – which continued the process of evangelisation. These churches, dotted all over Scotland from the Firth of Tay northwards, maintained strong links with the mother church on Iona, so strengthening the evangelical and diplomatic ties, and reducing the tension between the Picts and the Scots of Dàl Riada. With the northern Picts now Christian, nominally at least, and closely tied into the monastery on Iona, Columba's establishment on the island was more secure.

When King Conall of Dàl Riada died, Columba was deeply involved in the negotiations to select his successor, Àedàn mac Gabràin, and it was to Iona that Aìdàn went in 574, to be inaugurated by Columba on the Stone of Destiny, and become, in due course, perhaps the most significant king of Dàl Riada of that period. By then, however, tensions were increasing between the Scottish and Irish branches of Dàl Riada. And so in the year after his inauguration, Aìdàn and Columba attended the Convention of Kings at Druim Cett at Mullgach near the modern town of Limavady in County Londonderry/Derry. The Convention was a national assembly of princes, heads of tribes and clergy – in effect an embryonic parliament – and it was very powerful.

Two outcomes of that Convention are relevant to our understanding of Columba's importance in relation to the Stone of Destiny. The first was the settling of the differences which had been growing for some time between the Scottish and the Irish kings about the rights of the Irish kings to raise taxes and impose levies on the Scots. This agreement brought about the virtual independence of the Scottish Dàl Riada from the Irish kings.

Perhaps more important for our understanding of the fate of the Stone of Destiny, was the 'Staying of the Bards'. At that time the bards in Ireland, and in the Scottish Dàl Riada, enjoyed many privileges and immunities including access to the households of kings and chiefs. Nonetheless, over the years these privileges were increasingly abused, in particular by unreasonable demands for hospitality by the bards, and the chiefs and princes were threatening to withhold all the hospitality. Had that been withdrawn, the bardic culture would have withered from lack of support, and much of Irish and Scottish history might eventually have been lost. Columba negotiated restrictions on the demands of the bards, which safeguarded their role, and thus preserved a great Irish, and indeed a Scottish institution. Columba was clearly a man who valued history and tradition.

Nothing is known for sure about the Stone of Destiny for almost the next 200 years, and very little is known about the kings of Dàl Riada. Columba died in 597, and King Àedàn mac Gabràin in 606 but little is known about the kings who came after him. It is most likely that the Stone remained on Iona in the custody of St Columba's successors.

Columba's Relics Come to Mainland Scotland

In 795, almost 200 years after Columba's death, the first Viking raid on Iona took place. There had been Viking raids at other places in the Hebrides before that, and so Columbia's relics had already been moved to mainland Scotland for safety. There is no account of what these relics included or when exactly this happened and nor is there any record of where in Scotland they went. It was most probably the castle at Dun Monaidh, which was still an important base for the kings of Dàl Riada, and which by this time may already have been generally referred to as Dunstaffnage.

That said, it seems likely that the Stone of Destiny, and St Columba's relics were eventually taken to Dunadd, that volcanic pinnacle of rock piercing the raised peat bog of the Moine Mhor, the marshy lands around the River Add, a few miles east of Crinan. This had become the main administrative and military centre of the kings of Dàl Riada, superseding Dun Monaidh. Although it was the site of major fortifications, these would have been built mainly of wood, and little has survived. Nevertheless, visitors will find that there are excellent interpretation boards explaining what would have been there in the fifth century.

There is, however, one important ancient survival on Dunadd – a carved footprint in the bedrock at the summit of the pinnacle. It is likely that this would have been part of an ancient inauguration rite, such as those known to have been practised in Ireland and by the Lords of the Isles. The carved footprint was said to have been made for the foot of the first king or chief, and each subsequent would-be king, or chief-elect gave a solemn undertaking, as he fitted a foot into the carving, that he would preserve the ancient customs of his forebears. There was strong symbolism in this act of uniting the king with the land upon which everything depended.

Carved footprint in the bedrock at the summit of the pinnacle, Dunadd.

The Stone of Destiny Comes to Scone

By the first quarter of the ninth century, Scone was the royal centre of an ambitious tribe inhabiting the Pictish province of Fortriu which comprised the historic county of Perthshire and included the area around the Lake of Menteith. At that time the 'kings' of Fortriu had come to dominate the warlords and kings of all the provinces of Pictland from the Forth to the Pentland Firth. They had embraced Christianity in the seventh century, when monks from Iona set up a monastery at Scone, which eventually became Scone Abbey. By the eighth century, there was also a major Christian centre in Abernethy, an important palace at Forteviot as well as hill-forts at Dunkeld (King's Seat), at Dundurn in West Strathearn, on Moncreiffe Hill south of Perth, and Dunsinane Hill in Strathmore.

The events leading to the takeover of Pictland by MacAlpin are far from clear and there are a number of possibilities. What is certain is that by 843, the Picts had been seriously weakened in a catastrophic defeat by the Vikings in a battle in Strathmore (in 839), during which they lost most of their leaders and aristocracy. Perhaps the most likely of several traditions is that MacAlpin capitalised on this disaster and subdued the Picts in a treacherous betrayal of etiquette. He and his entourage had been invited to a banquet in Scone as guests of King Drust of the Picts. The Pictish nobles had drunk heavily, and, as the meal ended, MacAlpin and his warriors rose up and very quickly dispatched the Pictish king and most of his retinue. MacAlpin then acted swiftly to consolidate his hold on Pictland and, in due course, become the ruler of all of Scotland north of the Forth and Clyde.

John of Fordun states that, thereafter, King Kenneth MacAlpin brought the Stone of Destiny to Scone although no date is given, and he does not say whence it came. According to the *Pictish Chronicle*, the stone and the relics of St Columba were first brought to the east by MacAlpin, perhaps after a time in Kells in Ireland, 'in the seventh year of his reign', which would have been about 849/850. They were installed in a church by the River Tay, which had been founded for Columba by the King of the Picts in 570. This church may have been at Dunkeld on the site now occupied by Dunkeld Cathedral. Sometime later they were brought to the church in Scone, which, as noted above, had also been founded by monks from Iona. Later, of course, that church probably became Scone Abbey.

It is worth speculating on why Moot Hill was chosen by MacAlpin as his new royal centre. Clearly Dunadd was far away to the west from whence it would be quite difficult to effectively rule the important bulk of his new conquests in Pictland. Moreover, Scone was already the centre for the dominant Pictish province of Fortriu with whatever infrastructure that was appropriate for a Pictish king in the ninth century already in place. Even more important, from the point of view of maintaining his hold over the more far flung Pictish tribes, Scone's strategic location provided easy access to all of Perthshire, Fife and Angus. Furthermore, there were well-trodden routes west up the Earn valley to Argyll and his previous stronghold at Dunadd; north up the Tay valley to northern Scotland and Skye and northeast over the Mounth to Aberdeenshire. Meanwhile the Tay estuary facilitated access to the North Sea for MacAlpin's experienced sailors, which was important militarily to move men and materials rapidly to any area of conflict in the north, and it also unlocked the potential for trade with southern Britain and northern Europe.

The volcanic pinnacle of Dunadd dominates the flat (once marshy) land around it.

Additionally, on close examination of the landscape, it is clear that Moot Hill and Dunadd had a great deal in common – far more than is apparent now. If the relatively modern Scone Palace (dating originally

Scone Palace from the River Tay. The top of Moot Hill is just above the level of the highest windows, depriving the Palace of its strategic, cultural and psychological significance.

from the 1580s), along with the Mansfield Mausoleum and the large trees were swept away, the landscape surrounding Moot Hill would be seen to be quite similar to that around Dunadd. While it is a smaller mound than Dunadd, it stands on the top of a significant escarpment about 100 feet above what was a flat tidal marsh stretching north, west and south to a sweeping bend in the River Tay, very reminiscent of the marshy landscape surrounding Dunadd. In MacAlpin's time, a lookout on Moot Hill would have had a 360-degree view, south to the early settlement at Perth, west across the river to the Ochil Hills, north up the Tay valley, and east to the Sidlaw Hills. Furthermore, the approach to Moot Hill up the slope from the south was protected by the deep gully of the Catmoor Burn. There could have been few better lookout or defensive positions in the area, and none with the added significance of having been a Pictish Royal centre.

These very significant strategic factors led to the cultural, psychological and ceremonial importance of Moot Hill. It became the seat of royal power in Scotland, and the site of the inauguration of Scotland's monarchs for 700 years. Sadly, the landscape significance of Moot Hill is now greatly diminished. The enormous bulk of Scone Palace, which was built along the top of the escarpment, completely obscures Moot Hill from the River Tay, and so deprives it of its strategic and psychological importance. More recently, large trees have been planted on its slopes, further limiting the outlook and reducing its impact.

Myth or Legend?

At this stage it is important to distinguish between myths and legends. A 'myth' is defined in the *Oxford English Dictionary* as, 'a purely fictitious narrative', whereas a 'legend' is defined as, 'an unauthenticated story handed down by tradition, and popularly regraded as historical'. *How much of the story of the Stone of Destiny is 'purely fictitious myth' and how much is 'unauthenticated story, popularly regarded as historical'?*

The reports of the various stages of the Stone of Destiny's journey from Bethel, where Jacob had his dream, to Scone in Scotland must be treated with different degrees of scepticism. None of the chronicles tell us anything about the Stone from the time of Jacob until the time of the Biblical Exodus of the Jews from Egypt, when Moses, Scota, and Gaythelos all feature in the accounts, and the chronicles tell us that Scota secured the possession of the Stone. Indeed, the Stone of Destiny barely gets a mention until the time of King Milo and his son Simon Brecc in Galicia. By that time, however, the use of a stone 'throne' for royal inaugurations and judicial purposes was widespread among various Celtic peoples, and it is recorded that The Scots in Spain, although a separate and distinct tribe, conformed to this custom. While it is possible that it was just the concept of a royal stone that was imported from Galicia to Ireland and then to Scotland, the legends are unanimous although the details vary widely. The fundamentals are that The Scots in Galicia did have an actual stone throne or seat of justice, and that during one of the 'invasions' of Ireland from Galicia it was brought to Ireland and taken to the Hill of Tara, and in due course came to Scotland and became known as the Stone of Destiny.

While the Scottish and Irish chronicles concur that the Stone of Destiny was brought to Scotland from Ireland in 500, what it looked like, and from whence it came are very uncertain. *Was it Jacob's Pillow?*

Definitely not. *Did it come from Egypt?* Probably not, but then why in the Middle Irish poem, 'The Birth of Àidàn MacGabràin' was it referred to as the 'Eastern Stone'. *Was it a stone once used by the kings of The Scots in Spain?* Perhaps. *Was it delicately carved by skilled craftsmen?* We do not know.

What we do know is that The Scots in Spain were a distinct tribe, culturally if not genetically separate from the other Iberian peoples. Furthermore, what cannot be denied is that since archaeological, DNA and linguistic studies have tended to corroborate some of the most fundamental elements of the early legends with regard to the origin and travels of The Scots, it is cavalier to dismiss the many accounts of a revered symbol of their nationhood as totally without foundation – indeed as a 'purely fictitious narrative', in other words, as a myth. It is more appropriate to respect these accounts as 'unauthenticated stories, handed down by tradition and popularly regarded as historical', that is as legends, which may well have elements of truth embedded within them.

———————————

Chapter 4
The Appearance of the Stone of Destiny Before 1296

If the legends about the substitution of the Stone of Destiny by
Abbott Henry and his monks are true, what might the original
Stone of Destiny have looked like?

Legendary Descriptions

DESCRIPTIONS of the Stone of Destiny prior to its removal to London are regrettably rare, and there are no mediaeval illustrations of the Stone itself. Furthermore, the very earliest descriptions, those of the Stone brought from Galicia to Ireland by Simon Brecc, are ambiguous. As noted earlier in the first of John of Fordun's two accounts, the stone given to Simon Brecc by his father, King Milo, was marble, with exquisite carvings upon it. A precious and decorated stone is nothing more than you would expect for an icon belonging to a nation with a long and very powerful cultural tradition, and outstanding skills as stonemasons. Stone-age Galicians carved cup and ring marks similar to those found all over Scotland and Ireland, and later this flowered into elaborate religious art which can still be seen in the churches and cathedrals of Galicia. However, Fordun tells us neither the size nor shape of this stone. He does not mention its colour, nor does he describe the carvings that he says were on it. Nevertheless, the stone was obviously big enough to be used as a chair. In the second of Fordun's two accounts of Simon Brecc's stone, in which he tells how the stone was dragged up from the seabed, he merely described it as a block of marble 'cut in the shape of a throne'. He offers no explanation for the two mutually-exclusive descriptions.

Hector Boece's account of the appearance of a stone was written 150 years after John of Fordun, and draws on that chronicle, referring to a 'marble throne, or fatal stone as large as a seat', and adds a Latin inscription, as noted in Chapter 2, which can be translated as:

> The Scots shall hold that realm as native ground,
> If fates fail not, where'er this chair is found.

In other mediaeval accounts, including Walter Bower's *Scotichronicon*, the Stone is referred to as, 'this royal seat of stone', and in a thirteenth/early-fourteenth century English account by William Rishanger (*Chronica et Annales*) as, 'the stone which the Kings of Scotland were accustomed to use as a throne'. This is a little ambiguous because it is not absolutely clear whether the stone itself was the throne, or whether the stone was housed in a throne. George Buchanan, writing in *Rerum Scoticarum Historia*, in 1582 describes the stone as a 'marble rock', and states that King Kenneth MacAlpin had the stone 'enclosed in a throne of wood'. In none of the accounts of the appearance of the stone, and in particular, in none of the Scottish chronicles, all of which were written long after 1296, is there any comment on the obvious discrepancy between the descriptions given in the chronicles and the appearance of the stone taken by Edward's soldiers. That stone is not big enough to sit upon with dignity, nor is it shaped in any way like a chair or throne, and, furthermore, it is not decorated in any way. However, the simple explanation of this conundrum may be that none of the chroniclers would have seen the Stone in London, or indeed when it was in Scone Abbey, and as they were unaware that a substitution may have taken place, they assumed that the Stone which they had described was indeed that which had been taken to, and remained, in London.

The Inaugurations of Alexander III in 1249 and John Balliol in 1292

The first inauguration ceremony to be described in detail, both by John of Fordun and Walter Bower, was that of the boy-king Alexander III in 1249. Alexander's father, Alexander II, had died in his galley ship off the Island of Kerrera during a seaborne expedition to try to oust the Vikings from the Hebrides. Seven days later, on the 13th of July, his seven-year-old son was brought to Scone for the inauguration.

In John of Fordun's account, Alexander was led:

> up to the cross which stands in the graveyard at the east end of the church. There they set him on the royal throne which was decked with silken cloths inwoven with gold: the Bishop of St Andrews, assisted by the rest, consecrated him king as was meet. So the king sat down on the royal throne – that is the

stone – while the earls and other nobles, on bended knee, strewed their garments under his feet, before the stone. Now this stone is reverently kept in that same monastery for the consecration of Kings of Alba (Scotland): and no king was ever wont to reign in Scotland, unless he had first, on receiving the name of king, sat upon this stone at Scone, which, by the kings of old, had been appointed the capital of Alba. But lo, when all was over, a Highland Scot suddenly fell on his knees before the throne, and bowing his head hailed the king in his mother tongue, saying these words in Gaelic: 'Benach de Re Albanne, Alexander, MacAlexander, MacVleyham, MacHenri, MacDavid', and reciting it thus he read off even unto the end the pedigree of the Kings of Scots. This means in English: – 'Hail king of Alba, Alexander, son of Alexander, son of William, son of Henry, son of David'...

The recitation of the pedigree of the new king was an important and very ancient custom. It was read in Gaelic by the king's official bard, who was part of the king's retinue. By the time of Alexander III, the list amounted to thirteen generations back to Kenneth MacAlpin, then a further 43 generations covering eight centuries back to Fergus Mòr mac Eric, a total of 56 kings, and then even further back through the mythical kings to Scota and Gaythelos.

The only account of a royal inauguration at Scone written by a contemporary chronicler is that by Walter of Guisborough describing the inauguration of John Balliol. Walter was an Englishman, an Augustinian canon in the church of St Mary of Guisborough in North Yorkshire, and he was active as a chronicler from 1290 to 1305, precisely the period covering the inauguration, the invasion of Scotland by Edward I and the removal of the Stone of Destiny. He was mainly an historian of English events, from 1066 to 1346, and only mentions Scotland in detail when Scottish events affected England. This was obviously the case from 1290 with the death of Margaret, Maid of Norway, until 1314, and the Battle of Bannockburn. According to some accounts, Walter of Guisborough attended the inauguration of Alexander III himself, and he would certainly have known of, and may have been familiar with, Anthony Bek, the Bishop of Durham who, under Edward I's instruction. was the senior cleric officiating at the ceremony, in the place of the Bishop of St Andrews.

Balliol's inauguration was on the 30th of November, St Andrew's Day, 1292, and was the last inauguration to have been held on the Stone of Destiny in Scone. It was different from its predecessors in a number of ways, mainly because it was choreographed by Edward I, but also because it was held inside the Abbey church, rather than outside which was the normal custom. We do not know why the ceremony was normally held outside, but it may have been because the church was too small to accommodate the number of people expected to attend. Perhaps the most likely reason for altering the location of the ceremony to the inside of the church was that the weather was cold and wet, which is frequently the case at the end of November.

Walter of Guisborough begins his account of the inauguration in the monastery of Scone with the following description of the Stone on which the future kings were placed for their coronation, according to Scottish custom:

> In the church of God, near to the high altar, was an exceedingly large stone (*Lapis perigrandis in ecclesiae Dei juxta magnum altare*) which was hollowed out as a round chair (*concavus quidem ad modum rotundae cathedrae confectus*).

This is the full extent of his description of the Stone. Importantly, he does not mention its shape or colour, nor comment further on its size. He does not refer to any inscriptions or carvings upon it nor does he state whether or not it was enclosed in a wooden throne. In any case, it would probably have been covered with embroidered cloths which would have obscured these details. If Walter of Guisborough was indeed present in person, he would have been a fairly junior member of the English clerical team, and even if he had the inclination, it is unlikely that it would have been appropriate for him to investigate the Stone further, especially considering it was not in any way controversial at that time.

It is notable that when describing the Stone of Destiny, both Walter of Guisborough and John of Fordun use the Latin term *cathedrae*, which means a 'chair' and more usually describes a bishop's throne, rather than the word *sedes* which just means a 'seat'. It is worth emphasising Walter of Guisborough's usage of the Latin word 'cathedrae' and his statement that the Stone was 'exceedingly' large. No other description of the Stone emphasises its size in the same way. By no stretch of imagination can the Westminster stone fit this description. Other texts refer to the stone as 'the marbill chiar' and 'the regal chayre', none of which are compatible with a stone only 280 mm high. In order for the future king to retain his dignity, that stone would have to be elevated on legs, or a platform.

Significantly, the future king, John Balliol, was placed upon the throne, not by the Earl of Fife, who was an infant, nor by a member of the Earl's family, as would normally have been the case if the earl was unavailable, but by Sir John de St John, an English knight, and a nominee of Edward I. Furthermore, the officiating cleric was not the Bishop of St Andrews, as it had always been in previous inaugurations, but the Bishop of Durham, again on Edward's instruction.

Great Seals of the Kings of Scots

The nearest that we get to an actual pictorial representation of what the Stone of Destiny might have looked like, and in particular an indication of its size, is by an examination of the great seals of the mediaeval kings of Scots. Several of these survive dating from King Edgar, who reigned from 1097 to 1106, to King John Balliol (who was inaugurated in 1292). The seals are made of beeswax, with the obverse in every case showing the king mounted on a warhorse, usually with a sword, but sometimes with a banner, in his right hand. On the converse there is a representation of the king seated at his inauguration, robed and crowned. In every case, he has the Sword of State in his right hand and the Sceptre in his left.

In the aftermath of the raid on Westminster Abbey by the Glasgow students, and the flurry of interest in the Stone of Destiny that this caused, James S Richardson, formerly HM Inspector of Ancient Monuments of Scotland, published an important paper on the subject including a detailed study of these seals, to see whether they could shed any light on the size, shape, and decoration of the Stone of Destiny, and more importantly on its provenance.[1] It was published after the raid on Christmas Day, 1950, but

---

1 James S Richardson, 'The 'Stone of Destiny': Early Scottish enthronements', *The Scotsman* (17 February 1951).

*Obverse of the Great Seal of Malcolm IV
(reigned 1153–1185).*

before the Stone was returned to Arbroath Abbey, and it is the first publication in which a well-argued case is made for the substitution of the Stone of Destiny by the monks of Scone Abbey.

His conclusion found important support from the historian and writer, A C McKerracher, and the historical novelist, Nigel Tranter.[2]

The first of these seals, that of Edgar, though sadly much damaged and only one-sided, shows him seated on an X-shaped throne, encasing the Stone. The king is not robed, but the Stone is covered with a cloth, which falls down on all sides and obscures it.

In the royal seals struck from the beginning of the twelfth century to the middle of the thirteenth, Alexander I, David I, Malcolm IV, William the Lion and Alexander II, the king is shown sitting on a substantial cushion placed on what looks like a stool or chair without a back, presumably the Stone, with his feet on a shallow footstool. The king's legs and robes completely obscure the Stone, which was probably also covered, as John of Fordun related, with rich cloths embroidered with gold. While it is fair to say that the design of these later seals may be to some extent formulaic and influenced by English and Continental examples, all of them depict the king seated on a box-like throne without a back.

Some of the earlier seals show what appear to be metal hooks projecting from the base of the Stone. Richardson believed that these may have been carrying hooks. Several of them also show two round objects on either side of the throne. The significance of these is not known, but they will be discussed further in Chapter 14.

Only by the time of Alexander III does the seal show an elaborate

---

2 A C McKerracher, 'Where is the real Stone?' *Scots Magazine* (December 1984); Nigel Tranter, 'An Luath Fail - But Which Stone is that of Destiny?', *Scots Magazine* (August 1960).

Alexander I (reigned 1107–1124). Note the two tablets on either side of the throne.

David I (reigned 1124–1153).
Note the two tablets on either side of the
throne as with the Seal of Alexander I.

throne, probably more in keeping with European custom.

All of the thrones depicted in these seals would appear to accommodate a much bigger and heavier stone than that acquired by Edward I. Moreover, the illustrations of the thrones, although spanning a period of almost 200 years, all suggest a stone of the same size. There is a consistency about the illustrations of the shape and size of the throne, which is not matched by a consistency in the illustrations of the kings. A stone which would fit in one of the thrones, would fit them all.

Richardson's work on the seals suggests a Stone of around 420–508 mm in height and around 381–457 mm square, suggesting a volume of approximately 96 litres. This is very much more (approximately 30%) than the volume, and no doubt the weight, of the Stone of Scone, justifying Walter of Guisborough's description, 'lapis perigrandis'.

The shape and smaller size of the Stone of Scone highlight two issues. In the first place, it is too long to fit comfortably into any of the thrones depicted on the seals. At 670 mm long it is over 200 mm longer than the probable maximum width of the thrones, using Richardson's calculations. There is no indication in any of the seals of such a long stone being concealed beneath the rich cloths covering it. Secondly, with a height of only 265 mm, it would need to be

Malcolm IV (reigned 1153–1165).

William the Lion (reigned 1165–1214).

raised at least 150 mm to bring it to a height that would make a comfortable seat for a king. In every case, the seals appear to depict a seat which is high enough to have encased a taller stone and one of a different shape from that taken to London, and none of the seals show any evidence of supports to raise the Stone to a more appropriate height.

In every case, the seat of the throne is high enough to have encased a more substantial, and in particular, a much taller stone than the one taken to London. In some of the seals, it appears that the stone may be decorated by carving, and in all of them it seems to be resting on the floor, but enclosed in a wooden 'throne'.

In Westminster, the throne, which was specially constructed to hold the Stone of Destiny, is raised on four lion feet in order to lift it high enough to form a dignified seat for a king. None of the depictions of the seals show the Scottish throne raised in the same way. Unfortunately, none of the Scottish thrones survive, and in none of the depictions is it possible to get a clear idea of the actual appearance of the Stone itself because it is obscured by the king's legs and robes and by embroidered cloths as well. Indeed, in some of the seals it appears that the Stone is hidden behind a lattice screen.

Close examination of some of the seals suggests that there may be a

Alexander II (reigned 1214–1249).

Alexander III (reigned 1249–1286).

curved edge, or volute, on the lateral sides of the top of the Stone. This is not dissimilar to the curved edge on a Roman altar stone. Nigel Tranter was greatly influenced by Richardson's treatise on the great seals, and produced a sketch of what he thought the Stone might have looked like.[3] He includes in his sketch the curved lateral edge of the Stone, the concave seat, and intertwined Celtic designs. Tranter's sketch has been widely republished.

As well as examining the great seals of the kings of Scots, Richardson pointed out that all the early chroniclers described the Stone of Destiny as decorative and intricately carved, and elaborated how such antique sacred stones were nearly always made from meteorites, and were hard and able to take on a shiny polish. The stone taken by Edward I, is quite different being relatively soft sandstone, easily worked as a building material.

What Conclusions Can be Drawn from these Brief Texts and Ambiguous Illustrations?

Walter of Guisborough is the key witness. Because he was English, and because his account was contemporaneous, he was probably not influenced by the Scottish legends and the early chronicles (now lost)

3 Nigel Tranter, *Scotland: A Very Personnel Review* (Glasgow: Richard Drew Publishing, 1981).

Nigel Tranter's sketch of what the Stone of Destiny might look like.

which informed the accounts of John of Fordun, Walter Bower, Sir Thomas Grey and others, all of whom were writing very much later. For these reasons, his description of the Stone, brief though it is, is much the most important. As noted above, Walter of Guisborough described the Stone as 'exceedingly large' (*lapis perigrandis*), which is not consistent with the appearance of the stone uplifted by Edward I's soldiers, which is only 280 mm high and had to be housed in a throne raised up on four lion feet to enable the monarch to sit on it with dignity.

Was the Stone an Early Christian Artefact?

Nick Aitchison recounts various speculative possibilities to account for the origin, appearance and veneration of the Stone.[4] These include that it may have had connections with St Ninian in Whithorn, or St Boniface in the Black Isle, or Irish missionary saints. He also records the possibility that it was St Columba's Pillow, a suggestion which will be examined later. However, the underlying assumption in Aitchison's work is that there was no substitution by the monks of Scone Abbey, and that the stone currently on view is the stone venerated by the Picts since before the days of Kenneth MacAlpin and, thereafter, by the conquering Scots from Argyll.

---

4 Nick Aitchison, *Scotland's Stone of Destiny* (Cheltenham: The History Press, 2000). See also Chapter 11.

It is impossible to imagine that a block of Old Red Sandstone, quarried from near Scone could have connections with Whithorn, the Black Isle or Ireland. Moreover, there are no documented, legendary, folk, or even mythical memories supporting any of these possibilities, unlike the multitude of legends and folk memories relating to the Stone's origin in Galicia and its travels through Ireland to Scotland.

Was it a Roman Altar Stone?

The description of the Stone of Destiny as 'extremely large and hollowed out like a chair', and the fact that such a chair could have been accommodated by the thrones depicted on the great seals of the kings of Scots, have led a number of authorities to suggest that the original Stone of Destiny may have been a Roman altar stone. Several such altar stones are known to exist, and they are of approximately the right size and dimensions to fit the description. This idea was promoted by Richardson in February 1951, in his paper on the Stone of Destiny discussed earlier. The theory was also espoused by the journalist, Janet B Christie, and publicised by her in 1970 in *The Scots Magazine*[5]

Exhibit F.22 in the Hunterian Museum of Glasgow, which looks remarkably like a chair-like throne is cited as evidence for the theory.

Although square, the top of F.22 is rounded and hollowed out, rather like a font and was used for burning incense to the deities or the deified emperor identified on the pediment of the altar. Unfortunately, the pediment of F.22 is broken, but when complete, the altar stone would probably have been around 457 mm tall, and with a footstool, could have formed quite a dignified seat for a king. This particular altar stone (F.22)

Roman Altar Stone
(Exhibit F22, Hunterian Museum, Glasgow).

5 Janet B Christie, J B T, 'Doubts About "The Stone"', *Scots Magazine* (November 1970).

came from a shrine at the Castlecary Roman Fort near Falkirk, and was donated to Glasgow University in 1774, and there is no suggestion that it was ever the Stone of Destiny. The hypothesis is, however, that the Stone of Destiny was originally a similar Roman altar stone which could have come from a Roman shrine at the western end of the Antonine Wall, after the Romans withdrew from southern Scotland around 186.

The Antonine Wall runs from the north bank of the Clyde, near where Old Kilpatrick now is, to the Forth, and skirted the southern boundary of the territory controlled by The Scots. There were numerous Roman shrines along the wall, and it is postulated that an altar stone from one of them was gradually adopted as a religious or ceremonial icon by The Scots of Dàl Riada over the subsequent 200–300 years, and in due course taken to Scone by Kenneth MacAlpin.

The problem for this hypothesis is that there is no documentary evidence, nor folk memory supporting it. Furthermore, since the stone uplifted for Edward I in no way resembles a Roman altar stone, it must have been substituted by the monks of Scone Abbey, This hypothesis does not, therefore, bring us any closer to finding out what actually happened when Edward's soldiers came to Scone Abbey in 1296, and it does not lead to any conclusion about where the original Stone of Destiny, whatever its origin, might be. The only argument in favour a Roman altar stone is that it would fit the space in the throne as shown in the royal seals.

Was it Saint Columba's Pillow?

A number of stones from Iona have been the subject of somewhat far-fetched claims to have been St Columba's Pillow, and perhaps the Stone of Destiny. One nineteenth-century tradition relates to the Black Stones of Iona. The Black Stones stood near St Columba's tomb, and were not black in colour, but brought 'black doom' on anyone who violated an oath sworn over them. All these stones disappeared, one by one, during the first half of the twentieth century.

Another tradition dating from Victorian times is that the rough water-worn boulder with a carved cross and circle engraved upon it, now displayed in the Abbey church museum on Iona, was St Columba's Pillow. It had been dug up by a crofter in 1870 about 1 km north of the abbey and it became so popular that it had to be protected by an iron cage. However, further discoveries and modern research have shown that it is one of a number of cross-marked boulders found on Iona. The style of the cross with the circle dates this stone to the ninth century, some 200 years after Columba, and it is now thought that these stones may have been grave markers, or boundary stones. Those carved on both sides would have been upright, those carved on only one side, recumbent.

Aitchison discounts another suggestion that a local boulder which had been used by Columba as his pillow, was then set up as a grave marker, and that eventually this

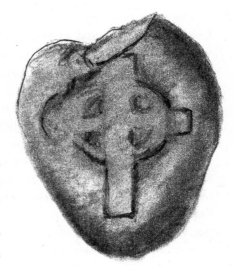

St Columba's 'Pillow'. Probably a grave marker or boundary stone.

became revered as the Stone of Destiny after it had been brought to mainland Scotland and then to Scone. He points out the obvious problem with this hypothesis, which is that a stone brought from Iona could hardly have been Old Red Sandstone sourced from Kincarrathie.

Did the Stone of Destiny Become St Columba's Pillow?

A more intriguing hypothesis suggests that contrary to the popular Victorian tradition that St Columba's Pillow became the Stone of Destiny, the converse is more likely, that the Stone of Destiny which had been brought to Iona for Àedàn mac Gabràin's inauguration, was then used by Columba as his pillow.

We are fortunate to have two biographies of Columba, by St Cumine the White and St Adomnàn, and both of them record the legend that Columba used a rock as his 'pallet', and a stone as his pillow, and that the latter became greatly revered. We have seen (in Chapter 3) how much Columba valued history and tradition. *With the Stone of Destiny on the Island of Iona since Aìdàn's inauguration, did Columba take possession of it, and keep it by his bedside, and was that how reverence for St Columba's Pillow began?*

The Stone of Destiny was already revered by the Celtic Scots among Columba's retinue, and its long-standing association with St Columba would also endear it to the Picts. Following his death in 597, this stone pillow was set up as a 'pillar' (to quote both his biographers) beside his grave, so clearly it was not a pillow in any modern sense of the word, but its size and shape was consistent with that of the Stone of Destiny. Sadly, neither of Columba's biographers included a description of St Columba's Pillow, and there is no other evidence to corroborate this hypothesis.

Columba, however, was greatly revered both by the Picts and The Scots, and had founded many churches in Pictland, and converted many of its important leaders to Christianity. While the Stone of Destiny was a Celtic tradition belonging to The Scots, St Columba's Pillow was a relic that would resonate very much with the Picts who made up a significant proportion of his entourage on Iona. Among several Pictish kings converted to Christianity by Columba was King Conal of the Picts who had built, in 570, a church on the banks of the Tay, probably the predecessor to Dunkeld Church and Cathedral. It is thought that it was to this church that Columba's relics were brought by Kenneth MacAlpin in 850, before moving them to Scone. If among the relics of St Columba was the Stone of Destiny, which had been used by Columba as his pillow, and which was revered by both the Picts and The Scots, then MacAlpin's objective to seek to integrate the two nations by installing this stone in Scone, was indeed an astute move.

What About Folk Memory?

Finally, should any weight be given to the folk memory, which is unanimous, that the stone was black, and probably basalt, and perhaps a meteorite; that it came, perhaps from Spain (or even the Middle East), but more likely from Ireland; and that it had been used to inaugurate the kings of the dynasty of Fergus Mòr mac Eric since 500 and perhaps before that. In Perthshire, in the 1930s, the Stone of Destiny was frequently referred to as, 'The Black Stone of Dunstaffnage'. The only sensible conclusion is that there is a serious disconnect between the descriptions of this stone and the appearance of the stone taken to Westminster. None of the descriptions in the chronicles, none of the representations on the seals, and certainly not the memory embodied in folklore, suggest that the stone used to inaugurate Scotland's kings up to John Balliol in 1292 looked anything like the stone uplifted for Edward I.

The inevitable conclusion must be that the real Stone of Destiny did not go to Westminster, and that Abbott Henry and the monks of Scone Abbey pulled off a remarkable deception, for which many of them would pay dearly when Edward's troops returned and ransacked the Abbey and tortured its priests in 1298.

Chapter 5
King Edward and the Stone of Destiny

THE MODERN HISTORY of the Stone of Destiny begins in 1296, at the culmination of the brutal subjugation of Scotland by Edward I of England, the Hammer of the Scots, and the utter humiliation of King John Balliol. Edward's rampage was an opportunist exploitation of the perceived weakness in Scotland following the accidental death of Alexander III, and the untimely death of his heir, Margaret, the Maid of Norway.

The reign of Alexander III had brought peace and prosperity to Scotland. Since he was enthroned on the Stone of Destiny at the age of seven in 1249, Scotland had enjoyed a golden age of relative peace while Edward was distracted by wars in Wales and expeditions to France, and had little inclination to pursue his claim to be overlord of Scotland. But it all came to an unexpected and dramatic end with the death of Alexander III. Alexander, aged 45, but old for his years, was under great pressure to produce a male heir. His first wife had died ten years earlier; their sons, Alexander, Prince of Scotland, and David, had died in 1284 at the age of twenty and in 1281 at the age of nine respectively; one of their daughters had died in infancy, and the other, Margaret, Queen of Norway, had died in 1283 in childbirth. However, her daughter, also called Margaret, the Maid of Norway, had survived.

A year earlier, Alexander had married for a second time and there were hopes that his new wife, Yolande de Dreux, would produce a male heir. And so, on the evening of the 18th of March he set off from Edinburgh to go home to Dunfermline. The weather was very stormy, and his friends pleaded with him to wait until the wind subsided. Even the ferryman at Queensferry refused initially to risk the crossing – but to no avail. He never arrived home, and the next morning, his body was found below the cliffs of Kinghorn.

In 1284, soon after the death of his son, Alexander, had called a Great Council of Scotland to meet in Scone. The conclusion was, that should he die without a male heir, his infant granddaughter would inherit the throne. And so, following protracted negotiations with her father, the King of Norway, who was initially unwilling to allow his seven-year-old

The Monument to Alexander III, near Kinghorn.

daughter to undertake such a perilous voyage across the North Sea, Margaret was put onto a Norwegian ship for the journey to Scotland and her kingdom. Sadly, it was the beginning of the autumnal stormy season, and by the time the ship arrived in Orkney, the child was mortally ill and died soon afterwards – it is said of seasickness. Her body was returned to Norway for burial in Bergen Cathedral. Although only seven, Margaret was already betrothed to Edward of Caernarfon, son and heir of Edward I. This would in due course have brought about the union of the Scottish and English Crowns and assured the English over-lordship of Scotland, which was Edward's driving ambition. There was now, however, no union of the Crowns on the horizon and so Edward, having subdued Wales, perceived an opportunity to extend his authority by force during a lull in his hostilities with France. The scene was set for the First War of Scottish Independence, a minor incident during which was the stealing of the Stone of Destiny from Scone Abbey.

Following the death of Margaret, the Maid of Norway, Scotland's senior cleric, William Fraser, Bishop of St Andrews, wrote to Edward, requesting that he choose one of a dozen claimants to the Scottish throne. The reason for this unlikely request was probably because the Bishop thought a decision by Edward would avoid a civil war between the main claimants, and also ensure peace with England. Consequently, in the summer of 1292, Edward came north to Norham, one of his major castles in Northumberland, to begin the protracted negotiations to choose Scotland's next king, called the Great Cause.

The two most prominent among a dozen aspirants for the throne were John Balliol and Robert Bruce, the 5th Lord of Annandale, known as 'The Competitor' on account of his longstanding claim to the throne. The Balliol and Bruce families were both descended from daughters of David, Earl of Huntingdon, the grandson of David I. Balliol was the grandson of Margaret, the elder daughter, while Bruce was the son of the younger daughter, Isabella. By this time, however, he was approaching 80. Because Balliol came from the elder sister, his claim was considered the stronger, although there was one more generation in his inheritance. He was eventually confirmed as the rightful heir to the throne of Scotland by a court of 140 auditors sitting in Berwick and presided over by Edward.

Shortly after this confirmation, Balliol swore fealty to Edward, and then rode to Scone where, on St Andrew's Day, 1292, he was inaugurated on the Stone of Destiny. Thereafter, with a minimum of delay, he went back south to Newcastle, where on the 26th of December he knelt, now as King of Scots, in homage to the English king, acknowledging Edward's overlordship over Scotland.

Meanwhile, in 1295, Robert Bruce, The Competitor's died, and his son, also Robert Bruce, the father of the future king, became 6th Lord of Annandale. However in 1296, he resigned his Lordship of Annandale and claim to the throne in favour of his son, and retired to his estates in Essex. Robert, the future king, was still only 22.

Edward's treatment of King John Balliol was humiliating at every turn. He treated him as no more important than one of his minor barons. The breaking point came in 1294 when Edward demanded men and money to continue his war with King Philip IV of France (Philip le Bel), and at the same time suppress an uprising in Wales. He summoned Balliol and demanded that he come to his aid with ten Scottish earls and sixteen barons, along with their retinues and finances to match. This was too much. At a meeting in Scone in July 1295, the leading Scottish nobles and clergy, along with the burgesses of the six most important burghs (of which Perth was one), responded by appointing a 'Committee of Twelve', four bishops, four earls and four barons, to demand that Balliol renounce his homage to Edward. Furthermore, in a flagrant challenge to Edward's

King John Balliol bends the knee in homage to Edward I.

authority, they began to negotiate a treaty of mutual support with France – the genesis of the Auld Alliance. This treaty was duly ratified by the French later in 1295, and by the Scottish Parliament, sitting in Dunfermline, in February 1296.

Outraged, Edward reacted swiftly, and on the 28th of March that year he crossed the border at Coldstream. He massacred the inhabitants of Berwick, defeated the Scots army at Dunbar, and then rampaged through Scotland spreading death and destruction as far north as Moray. Balliol was captured in a churchyard near Stracathro (in Angus) and surrendered to Bishop Anthony Bek who had conducted his inauguration only eight years earlier. In Brechin Castle, he was forced to repudiate the treaty with King Philip of France, which had been ratified by Parliament only a few months earlier, and abdicate. The Arms of Scotland were torn off the back of his robes, earning him the epithet 'Toom Tabard' – 'empty coat'. He was then imprisoned in the Tower of London, though later exiled to a comfortable retirement in his ancestral estate in Picardy.

On his way back to England, Edward stayed for the night of the 7th of August at Baledgarno, near the village of Inchture in the Carse of Gowrie. His next stop was Perth on the 8th of August, but before crossing the Tay he instructed his lieutenants to uplift the Stone of Destiny and take it to London. Edward also confiscated Scotland's emblems of State – the Crown, the Mace and the Sword of State, many of the nation's archives and stole the Black Rood of St Margaret, a reliquary which was said to contain a fragment of the true cross. All of these were eventually taken to London, where, in due course, the Stone of Destiny was incorporated into a specially-constructed throne in Westminster Abbey.

This theft gave rise to the first of a number of conundrums about the authenticity of the Stone of Destiny. *Was the stone that was removed by Edward's soldiers the real Stone of Destiny, or had the monks of Scone Abbey exchanged it for a block of local sandstone?* If it was indeed the Stone of Destiny, around which so much legend and myth had accumulated, it is strange that it was such an unprepossessing object. Certainly, Edward, who may have seen the Stone of Destiny during his previous expeditions to Scotland, did not himself supervise its removal, but it is a little surprising that none of his courtiers, some of whom would have undoubtedly been present at the inauguration of John Balliol in 1292, alerted him to the deception. However, that event took place inside the Abbey adjacent to Moot Hill at the end of November, and the light inside the church at that time would have been very poor. Moreover the stone, housed in a wooden 'throne', would have been draped in rich, gold embroidered cloths, and perhaps concealed behind a lattice framework. Under these circumstances Edward's courtiers probably did not notice it. They would have had other things on their minds besides inspecting this unprepossessing artefact belonging to a subdued nation.

It is possible that when Edward saw the stone after it arrived in London in 1297, he realised that he had been deceived. He had already ordered his goldsmith, Master Adam, to make a bronze throne for the Stone of Destiny, but the work had just started when Edward cancelled the order, and instead instructed his carpenter, Master Walter, to make a wooden chair. The most likely reason for this change of plan was not that Edward thought that a bronze throne was not worthy of an object of uncertain provenance, but cost. Expeditions to Scotland were expensive, and he was hard-up. He also declared that this new chair was not to be used by the king at coronations, but by the priest who was conducting the ceremony. That instruction, of course, was not fulfilled and the stone in its wooden throne has been used for all coronations since.

At the same time, he ordered a further expedition to Scone which, on the 17th of August 1298, resulted in serious damage to the Abbey:

> The ceilings, doors and windows of the church, the cloisters
> and the chambers were all smashed down; cupboards chests
> and caskets all broken open.

It is said that not one stone was left on another and that some of the monks were tortured. *Were they looking for the real Stone of Destiny?* If so, they did not find it.

Peace with England: The Treaty
of Edinburgh-Northampton

Hostilities between England and Scotland rumbled on and were not concluded by Bruce's victory at Bannockburn. Edward I died in 1307 on the banks of the Solway Firth looking over to Scotland which he hoped his son would conquer. However, he was not blessed with heirs of his stature and charisma. His son, Edward II, signally failed in battle at Bannockburn, and thereafter had been unable to protect his Northumbrian landowners from incursions by the Scots. These were probably sanctioned by King Robert the Bruce in order to exert pressure on the English Parliament. Meanwhile, machinations within the royal court at Westminster resulted in Edward II being deposed by his wife, Queen Isabella, and her lover, Roger de Mortimer; later, in 1327, he was murdered. His son, Edward III, was crowned in Westminster Abbey on the Stone of Destiny soon after, but he was only fourteen, and royal power remained with the ambitious Mortimer and officially with Isabella, now the Queen Mother.

The First War of Independence, which had begun in 1296, was ended finally by the Treaty of Edinburgh-Northampton. The negotiations which preceded this treaty began in York in 1324 during the reign of Edward II, with the presentation of Scotland's demands, which included the recognition of King Robert as the sovereign independent King of Scotland, and rejected all English claims of overlordship. By the Spring of 1328, negotiations in Northampton had reached a conclusion, and the Peace Treaty of Edinburgh-Northampton was signed by Robert the Bruce in Edinburgh on the 17th of March 1328, and ratified by the English Parliament, meeting in Northampton on the 4th of May 1329. By the treaty, the independence of Scotland was finally recognised – 'separate in all things from the Kingdom of England' – and Edward III finally recognised Robert the Bruce as the undisputed King of Scots. While the two nations had conducted the negotiations as equals, there is no doubt that the English monarchy had conceded, for the peace that followed was called the 'Shameful Peace', and Mortimer rapidly fell out of favour and was executed by hanging in 1330.

As one of the conditions of the treaty, the Scottish delegation had demanded the return of the Stone of Destiny. Initially, in 1324, the English negotiators rejected this demand, noting that the Stone of Destiny, 'had been taken as a sign of victory, and if we were to restore it we would seem basely to repudiate the right thus acquired'. Thereafter, the Stone of Destiny is not mentioned in the treaty – but it was not forgotten. Soon after the treaty was ratified, Edward III (acting doubtless on behalf of his mother) issued two writs. The first instructed the Abbott of Westminster to deliver the Stone of Destiny to the Sheriffs of London, and the second ordered the Sheriffs to have it taken to Berwick-upon-Tweed, and delivered to Isabella, the Queen Mother. The reason for her presence in the North of England was to negotiate the return of lands in Scotland that were owned, prior to the War of Independence, by Englishmen and forfeited by Robert the Bruce. There is no doubt that the Stone of Destiny was to be used as a bargaining counter. However, her plans came to nothing. It is said that the London mob, incensed by the English capitulation in the 'Shameful Peace', did not want to see this important emblem of their victory lost, and they prevented its removal. It is also likely that both the Abbott of Westminster and the Sheriffs of London were complicit in this stratagem. Royal prestige in England was low at this time, with divided loyalties, and Isabella was unable to assert her authority, and so the Stone of Destiny remained in Westminster.

The fact that Bruce did not pursue the matter further may have been because he was already a very sick man, confined mostly to bed in his castle at Cardross overlooking the Clyde. By the time news reached him that the English Parliament at Northampton had confirmed the treaty, he had barely a month to live before he died peacefully on the 7th of June. On the other hand, his failure to pursue the matter may have been because he did not think that it was important because he knew the stone in Westminster was a counterfeit.

The next occasion when the Stone of Destiny featured in negotiations between England and Scotland was in the aftermath of the Treaty of Berwick, which, in 1357, concluded the protracted Second War of Scottish Independence. It was a somewhat unlikely, even bizarre settlement, but the return of the Stone of Destiny to Scotland was promised – although with conditions. This Second War which had begun in 1332 and dragged on for 25 years was characterised by shifting fortunes, with dominance swinging north and south across the border. Furthermore, it also implicated the French, and, in 1337, it was complicated by the start of the Hundred Years War between England and France.

Following an English invasion of France in 1346, King Philip IV of France invoked the terms of the Auld Alliance and persuaded the Scots to invade the north of England. The Scots caused a great deal of destruction but their army was surprised at Neville's Cross and defeated, and David II was captured. He was held as a hostage in England for the next nine years until his return was secured at the Treaty of Berwick after the Scots agreed to pay a crippling ransom of 10,000 marks a year for the next ten years. When the Scots defaulted, Edward III proposed that the rest of the ransom would be waived if King David died childless (he was already in his mid-thirties), and if that happened, the Scots would accept the English king as King of Scots. It was to be a complicated arrangement. The two countries were not to be united, but the king would be crowned twice, once in London, and then again in Scotland, and the Stone of Destiny was to be returned permanently for the purpose. The deal, however, was rejected by the Scottish Parliament meeting in Scone in 1364, and the Stone of Destiny remained in London.

Thereafter, the Stone of Destiny seems to have slipped quietly from the public consciousness for the next 700 years, except for a brief but exciting excursion back to Scotland in 1950–1.

———————————————

Chapter 6
The Inauguration of King Robert the Bruce:
Was it on the Stone of Destiny?

THE AMBITION OF the Bruce family to take the Crown of Scotland was longstanding, but the actual claim was precipitated by the murder, by Bruce, of Sir John 'the Red' Comyn in the sanctuary of the Greyfriars Church, located a few miles outside Dumfries.

The year 1304 was a time of shifting intrigues and systemic treachery in Scotland. Notwithstanding that Bruce had sworn fealty to Edward I, and acknowledged his overlordship of Scotland on the 4th of June of that year, he had secretly secured a pact with Bishop William de Lamberton, the most prominent cleric in Scotland who had succeeded William Fraser as Bishop of St Andrews on the latter's death in 1297. Lamberton agreed to support a Bruce claim for the throne principally because of his concern that, with English rule, the church in Scotland would be brought under the control of the Archbishop of York. At that time, while the Bishop of St Andrews was the most senior bishop in Scotland, there was no archbishopric at the apex of the religious hierarchy.[1] The Church in Scotland was considered to be a 'Special Daughter of the See of Rome', and it was administered by the National Council of the Scottish Clergy, responsible directly to the Vatican. However, there was pressure from London on the Vatican to bring it under English control, and it was vulnerable. Lamberton wanted to see Scotland remain ecclesiastically, as well as politically, separate from England.

A little later, Bruce made another pact, this time with John Comyn, who had also sworn allegiance to Edward, but who agreed to support Bruce's claim for the throne in return for a promise of lands and privileges. This would reduce the threat to Bruce from the Balliol faction, many of whom were Comyn's close relatives. This deal was signed and sealed but the document remained in Comyn's possession. In January 1306, however, Comyn decided to betray Bruce, and informed Edward about the pact.

Edward, aware that he was being deceived, secretly sent emissaries to

---

1 St Andrews became an archbishopric in 1472.

Scotland to get the document which he intended to use to challenge Bruce. Meanwhile, Bruce, who was staying at Edward's court in London, got wind of the development and decided to flee back home to Scotland. On the way, he happened to meet the emissaries bringing Comyn's document to London. Bruce now had evidence of Comyn's treachery. A meeting to discuss their differences was arranged between the two men. This took place on the 10th of February 1306 in Greyfriars Church. It is believed that a holy place was chosen because it would be safer for both parties.

The meeting between the two rivals (and a couple of supporters for each of them) got underway in the church. After a while, Bruce and Comyn withdrew from the group to the sanctuary for greater privacy. Harsh words were suddenly exchanged and both men reached for their daggers. Bruce struck first and Comyn fell, mortally wounded. The rest of the group burst in and an uncle of Sir John, Robert Comyn, drew his sword and attacked Bruce. However, his assault was deflected by Bruce's armour, and the assailant was immediately attacked and killed by Christopher Seton, Bruce's brother-in-law. Bruce and Seton staggered out of the church, and Bruce said, 'I doubt I have slain the Red Comyn'. Roger Fitzpatrick, one of Bruce's entourage, responded, 'Do you doubt? Then, I'll mak siccar!', and he entered the church and finished off the Red Comyn.

The murder of Sir John Comyn rendered Bruce's situation extremely perilous. To have killed his rival in the sanctuary of a church was a terrible sin which would shock friends and enemies alike. Bruce was fortunate, however, to have secured the friendship and support of two of the most important clergymen in Scotland, Robert Wishart, the Bishop of Glasgow, and William Lamberton. These important connections would help him to gain the favour of the clergy and would enable him to brave the dreadful consequences of the sentence of excommunication which the Pope was almost certain to pronounce when the news of the dreadful desecration of the sacred environment of the church reached Rome.

Bruce rode immediately to Glasgow to seek absolution for his sin from Bishop Wishart. This was granted on the grounds that if he had not killed Comyn first, Comyn would have killed him, and thereafter Wishart sent word to the clergy around the country to rally them to the Bruce cause.

Although his supporters were few, Bruce then went directly to Scone to meet Bishop Lamberton and make his claim for the throne. As he travelled first to Glasgow and then on to Scone, he must have wondered if an inauguration could possibly be considered authentic.

There were two important elements in the traditional inauguration ceremony for a new mediaeval King of Scots. The first was the presence of the Chief of Clan MacDuff, the Earl of Fife. As noted earlier, the chiefs of Clan MacDuff had inherited the ancient Gaelic title of *Mormaor* or High Steward from the time of the MacAlpin dynasty, and with it came the right to inaugurate each new King of Scots, by placing him on the Stone of Destiny. Should the Chief not be available, one of his sons could deputise officially. The second requirement, of course, was the Stone of Destiny. A third element, at that time a modern development among European nations which had not been part of any previous inauguration in Scotland, was the anointing with Holy Oil by the most senior bishop in the land. This signified the transmutation of the King-elect to a new exalted status by an infusion of divine grace, and confirmed the legitimacy of the rite in the eyes of the Pope and the Church in Rome.

Fearing that he might be excommunicated, speed was essential, because once the Pope had issued an order of excommunication, Bishop Lamberton would be unable to officiate at the ceremony of anointment. But that was only one of the uncertainties. Another was the presence of the Chief of Clan Duff, who was unfortunately a hostage in London and his two sons were with him. And *what of the Stone of Destiny? Was it also a missing element, or was it brought out of hiding for this important occasion, which would emphasise Bruce's authority as the rightful king?*

There is a strong tradition that Abbott Henry, who was the Abbott of Scone Abbey when Edward's soldiers stole the Stone of Destiny eight years previously, would have known if the Stone had been substituted, and if so where it was hidden, and so he would have been able to produce it for the occasion. In the first volume of Nigel Tranter's trilogy of historical novels about Bruce (fictional, though based on extensive research) – *The Steps to the Empty Throne* – Bruce was unaware that the Stone had been saved until he was taken to see it in a crypt by a delighted Abbott Henry. That the Stone was produced is supported by records which claim that Bruce was inaugurated, according to John of Fordun, '*in sede Regali*' ('on the royal seat').

The third element, the ecclesiastical part of the inauguration ceremony, was the consecration of the new king which emphasised the close connection between the Church in Rome and the Scottish State.[2] This was conducted by the senior cleric in Scotland – the Bishop of St Andrews. Bruce was indeed fortunate that his friend and ally, William Lamberton, occupied that position.

With two of the three elements in place, (the Stone of Destiny and the Bishop of St Andrews, but without the Chief of Clan MacDuff), the ceremony could go ahead.

With his Anglo-Norman pedigree, Bruce was well aware that while the Celtic custom of inauguration on the Stone of Destiny was the tradition in Scotland, crowning was normal in England and in much of Europe, and he wished to ensure that the ceremony establishing his authority as the rightful King of Scots would be recognised as widely as possible. And so he had ensured that a circlet of gold was procured by Bishop Robert Wishart, and that he was crowned according to European tradition as well as being inaugurated according to the Celtic rite. It is said that Bishop Wishart also produced kingly robes and vestments which he had hidden away, 'until this longed for day dawned'. Sadly, the circlet of gold was lost to the English in the aftermath of Bruce's defeat at the Battle of Methven a few weeks later, and never recovered.

The ceremony took place in the Abbey church at Scone on Palm Sunday, the 25th of March 1306. Abbott Henry presided while the Sacrament was dispensed and the consecration of the new king was carried out according to the Scottish rite by Bishop Lamberton. The event is described, as noted above, with a modest amount of journalistic licence by Nigel Tranter.

On the next day, however, before Bruce and his company had left Scone, they were surprised by the sudden arrival of Isabella, the nineteen-year-old Countess of Buchan, the sister of the Earl of Fife, who had

---

2 Anointing with holy oil, which the Scottish kings had craved since Alexander II, and which signified the transmutation of the King-elect to a new exalted status by an infusion of divine grace and confirmed the legitimacy of the rite in the eyes of the Church in Rome, was not sanctioned for use in Scotland by the Pope until 1329, just before the death of Bruce. This rite was conducted for the first time in Scotland at the inauguration Robert's seven-year-old son, David II.

come to claim her family's privilege of placing the new king on the inaugural stone. For Isabella, a romantic and high-spirited young woman and a loyal supporter of the Bruce cause, her family's privilege trounced marital loyalty. She had deserted her husband, who was one of Sir John Comyn's near relatives and adhered to the Balliol faction, taken his horses, and with a few supporters had ridden to Scone, only to find that she was too late. She had missed the occasion by a day.

However, the Countess of Buchan was not a lady to be ignored, especially when her participation fulfilled one of the important traditions of the ceremony, and so Bruce was inaugurated for a second time on the 27th of March by being placed on the Stone of Destiny by Isabella, the Countess of Buchan, representing her father, the Earl of Fife, the Chief of Clan MacDuff.

This important event is illustrated in a stained-glass panel now in the possession of Lodge Scoon and Perth No 3, one of the oldest Masonic lodges in Scotland, at 5 Charlotte Crescent, Perth.[3] It was made as a special exhibit for the 1901 Glasgow International Exhibition, by David Gauld, one of the 'Glasgow Boys' circle of artists. The panel shows the king kneeling to receive the Host from Bishop Lamberton; behind is Bishop Wishart of Glasgow. Standing, holding the circlet of gold, is Isabella, Countess of Buchan.

Isabella was to pay dearly for her loyalty. Following Bruce's defeat at the Battle of Methven, she was captured and imprisoned for four years in a cage in the Castle of Berwick-upon-Tweed, and thereafter banished to the Carmelite friary in Berwick.

---

3 The exhibition records and an examination of the panel indicate that originally the panel had five sections. Four of them were given to the Lodge in 1930, but the one on the extreme left is missing. The Lodge would welcome any information about its whereabouts.

Chapter 7
The Raid on Westminster Abbey

FOR SIX AND A HALF CENTURIES, the Stone of Destiny lay in its oaken throne in Westminster Abbey, almost unnoticed except for occasional coronation ceremonies. And then, early on Christmas Day, 1950, a Sunday, the unthinkable happened. In a daring exploit by a group of four Glasgow students the Stone of Destiny was 'clandestinely removed' from the Abbey, to quote the Attorney General's careful choice of words in his statement to Parliament.

Even with the hindsight of more than 70 years, it is a remarkable story, and it has been well told by Ian Hamilton in his book, *No Stone Unturned*. The amateur nature of their organisation was matched by the inadequate security at Westminster, the incompetence of the subsequent police operation overseen by Scotland Yard, and the failure by both politicians, the police and the Abbey authorities to appreciate the divergent attitudes to the event on the different sides of the border. In England, although the population generally was fairly tolerant, the political and clerical establishments were scandalised by the sacrilegious violation of the very epicentre of the Empire, and this view was reflected by the London press. In Scotland, by contrast, the *Boy's Own Paper* nature of the exploit appealed to many people, including even to some elements of the aristocracy. They were amused to see the high and mighty dignity of the Church and State in London pricked by an altruistic group of young Scottish nationalists, whose daring exploit had righted an ancient wrong and had caused no one any injury.

Ian Hamilton, a 25-year-old law student at Glasgow University, was the leader of the group. He had dreamed of returning the Stone of Destiny to Scotland since childhood. However, enterprises such as this need help from various sources. Two members of the Glasgow establishment came on board at the start. The first was John MacCormick, lawyer, founder of the Glasgow University Scottish Nationalist Association, promoter of the Scottish Covenant, and at that

* * *

time, the Lord Rector of Glasgow University.[1] MacCormick introduced Hamilton to Bertie Gray, a Glasgow stonemason and businessman, the vice-chairman of the Scottish Covenant Association, and a bailie on Glasgow City Council. Both MacCormick and Gray had been involved in a previous attempt to retrieve the Stone of Destiny in the early 1930s, and Gray had made at least one replica of the Stone in his monumental mason's yard in Glasgow which he exhibited in his shop window. As well as providing level-headed advice and assistance, both men contributed financially to the enterprise.

Over a period of a few days at the beginning of Glasgow University's Christmas holiday in 1950, Hamilton gathered three accomplices. Kay Mathieson was the first. A native Gaelic speaker, she was training to be a teacher and was deeply involved in the National Covenant movement. Gavin Vernon was the next recruit, a 24-year-old engineering student, and then at the last moment, Alan Stuart, only twenty, and also a student at Glasgow University.

It is fascinating, to read the account of the operation from the perspective of the twenty-first century – much colder weather, no dual carriageways or bypasses round towns and cities, poorly signposted roads, no heaters in the cars, no electronic gadgets, and certainly no mobile phones. The four students drove down in two old, under-powered Ford Anglias – one hired and the other belonging to Alan Stuart. They arrived in London in the afternoon of the 23rd of December 1950. Hamilton had 'cased the joint' some months earlier, but a more detailed reconnoitre was required, so the four of them paid for admission. They went round the Abbey in two pairs so as not to arouse suspicion and examined every detail of security including the doorways, the locks and the security around the throne.

Although they were tired having driven the 400 miles from Glasgow, eighteen hours non-stop, they decided to make an immediate attempt to get the Stone the Destiny. Hamilton, who was well-equipped with a set of burglary tools, including a large jemmy which he hung round his neck

---

1 The Scottish Covenant was an early sign of the developing independence movement in Scotland. It was a petition to the UK government seeking 'Home Rule'. Resonating with the National Covenant of 1638, and the Ulster Covenant of 1912. It was initiated by John MacCormick and written in October 1949. It was eventually signed by two million people, though with little political effect.

and which extended down into his trouser pocket, entered the Abbey again before closing time and hid under a trolley, with the idea of opening the door of the Poets' Corner from the inside. However, he was caught by a nightwatchman, but was able to persuade him that he had been shut in by accident, and remarkably, he was released without having to identify himself. The group then spent the rest of the freezing night in the two cars. Outside that night it was – 10 °C.

By the afternoon of the next day, Kay Mathieson was coming down with the flu, and so they decided to get her a bed 'for the night' in a cheap hotel and return and pick her up when they were about to make the next attempt to get the Stone. The three men then spent some time investigating the area around the outside of an external door of the Abbey which lead to the Poets' Corner. During this time, Vernon and Stuart had another encounter with a nightwatchman, and were able to find out not only the location of the nightwatchman's office (and it was a long way from the throne) but also the rough times that he did his rounds of the Abbey – so it was a very valuable chance meeting.

That night, Saturday, Christmas Eve, 1950, was to be the night. There were no watchnight services in those days, even in the most prestigious churches. They spent the earlier part of the night breaking the lock to gain entry to the mason's yard which lay outside of the door of Poets' Corner, which they would have to force open later to enter the Abbey. Then, just before 3 am, they went back for Kay. Unfortunately, they had to hammer on the door of the hotel to raise the night staff, who then became suspicious and telephoned the police. In due course, a police car came round and a policeman asked them what they were doing. Fortunately, as it was Christmas Eve, he was in an amiable mood and so after checking Hamilton's driving licence and the registration of the old Anglia, he drove off. However, that was potentially a disastrous encounter, because not only was Hamilton now identified with the scene and time of the forthcoming 'crime', so also was the car. They presumed that once the alarm was raised, every policeman in London and farther afield would be on the lookout for that particular car, and that Hamilton would be a marked man.

They prepared to enter the Abbey soon after 3 am on Christmas Day. The older Anglia was left in a nearby car park and Kay remained on the road adjacent to the mason's yard in the other 'get-away' Anglia, which was as yet unidentified by the police. The three men forced the Poets' Corner door with Hamilton's jemmy and then made their way in pitch darkness to the throne containing the Stone of Destiny. They pulled and pushed the Stone of Destiny from its place beneath the seat of the throne, and then bumped it down the steps of the High Altar before dragging it towards the door. Hamilton took a hold of one of the iron rings and pulled. To his horror and dismay the Stone of Destiny broke into two pieces, a large corner of it coming away with the ring. 'We've broken Scotland's luck', a horrified Alan Stuart whispered. However, even by the light of a hand torch, they could see that the Stone of Destiny had a major fault and had obviously been cracked for a very long time. It appeared that it had only been held in one piece by a thin strip of the Stone at the top surface. Vernon and Stuart manoeuvred the larger piece onto Hamilton's coat and continued to drag it to the door at the Poets' Corner, while Hamilton then took the smaller piece out to the car where Kay Mathieson was waiting, and put it in the boot.

As Hamilton reached the car, Kay noticed a policeman approaching. She and Hamilton pretended to be lovers and complained to the policeman that they could not find a bed and breakfast place for the night. Luckily, once more, the policeman was affable and happy to chat for some time while he smoked a cigarette before wishing them on their way. Nonetheless, both cars had now been seen by the police, although it did not seem that Kay's Anglia had had its registration number noted, and neither occupant had been identified by the policeman. Hamilton decided that Kay should take the smaller part of the Stone of Destiny and drive to a friend's house in Birmingham, and there try to conceal the car and the Stone before the hue and cry got up. He drove off with her for a reasonable distance, then got out and walked back to the Abbey while she drove on to Birmingham. Unluckily, on her way through London she heard a crash as her part of the Stone of Destiny fell out of the boot, which Hamilton had not locked properly, and landed in the middle of the street. Kay got out of the car and lifted the fragment which weighed 41 kg (90 lbs – about her own weight) back into the boot and locked it securely. No one noticed or challenged her.

Meanwhile, Hamilton walked back to the Abbey. When he got there, the Stone of Destiny was lying on his coat in the builders' yard but there was no sign of Vernon or Stuart. He went to find the second car; it was still in the car park but still there was no sign of his accomplices. He realised that his friends did not have a key for the car and that he had lost his key, the only one, and that it had been in the pocket of his coat which had been used to drag the stone through the Abbey. And so, after checking his coat pockets, he went back to the Abbey, and on his hands and knees with the light from matches, he felt his way back to the throne. Remarkably, he found the key, and went back and brought the car round to the builders' yard. Then single-handedly, he proceeded to drag the large piece of the Stone out of the yard and loaded it into the old Anglia by himself. It was a remarkable feat, for this part of the stone weighed about 117 kg (246 lbs, nearly 18 stones), twice his own weight. He said, 'I felt the hands of God were over mine when I lifted the Stone'.

By this time – it was about 6 am – Hamilton was driving through the back streets of London trying to find the route south to Kent, when by another remarkable twist of fate, he met Vernon and Stuart walking dejectedly and aimlessly along the street. They had thought that he and Kay had been taken into custody by the policeman. It was exactly at this time, when the nightwatchman did his last round, that the alarm was raised in the Abbey.

Fearing that roadblocks would be set up on the roads north, Hamilton, Vernon and Stuart decided that it would not be sensible to drive the Stone of Destiny back to Scotland. They also decided to split up so that not all three of them would be apprehended at once. Vernon got out and a rendezvous was arranged. And so that Christmas morning, Stuart and Hamilton drove south, but expecting to be apprehended at any minute, they dumped the Stone of Destiny in an open field. A little later, emboldened by the absence of any police activity, they returned and retrieved it, and hid it more securely at the edge of a field a couple of miles out of Rochester.

Vernon did not make the rendezvous and they discovered later that he had become convinced that he was being followed by a plain-clothes policeman. Try as he might, he could not shake the man off so, not wanting to implicate the others, he returned to Scotland by train. Meanwhile Hamilton and Stuart, after spending some time waiting for

Vernon, set off for Scotland, stopping occasionally for some sleep and sustenance and to send a map of the Stone's location to Glasgow – just in case. They were pulled over at a police checkpoint on only one occasion, and they quickly realised that the police were unaware that their car had been seen and recorded outside the hotel where Kay was sleeping on the night of the raid. They pressed on with growing confidence that they would manage to get to Scotland safely.

Meanwhile, Kay looked up her friend, who although surprised to see her gave her a welcome and allowed her to put the car in her garage. She even believed the unlikely story that Kay told her to explain her sudden arrival on Christmas morning.

Her friend's family was having a guest for Christmas lunch – the Chief Constable of Birmingham! When the news came through at one o'clock, Kay said that her paper hat nearly flew off her head, but she kept her nerve, and later went back to Glasgow by train, leaving the car and the smaller part of the Stone of Destiny concealed and safe in the garage in Birmingham.

This was a wise choice as the border with Scotland was closed for the first time in 400 years, and off-duty policemen from across the Midlands and the north of England were summoned from their Christmas dinners to set up road blocks and search for the Stone of Destiny, which by then was safe in a field 50 miles south of London.

The next morning, Boxing Day, the enormity of what had happened hit the English establishment like a sledgehammer. Detectives and policemen from Scotland Yard flooded north and soon homed in on Glasgow and Edinburgh Universities. The hyperbole of the reaction in London, however, was not matched in Scotland. Some Scots, of course, were horrified at the violation of the sacred environment of Westminster Abbey, but many were elated, and most of the rest were quietly amused at the shock-horror of the statements emanating from the clerical and political hierarchies in London. The Scottish reaction was encapsulated in a remark by a middle-ranking Scottish policeman who said, 'Aye, sure we are looking for the Stone, but not so damned hard that we will find it', and in the irreverent ditty, by Johnny McAvoy, 'The Wee Magic Stane', sung by Robin Hall and Jimmy MacGregor, and banned for a while by the BBC.

The Wee Magic Stane

The Dean o' Westminster was a powerful man
He held a' the strings o' the State in his hand
But wi' a' his great business it flustered him nane
When some rogues ran awa' wi' his wee magic stane

Wi' a too-ra-li-oo-ra-li-oo-ra-li-ay

The Stane had great powers that could dae sic a thing
That withoot it it seemed we'd be wantin' a king
So he sent for the polis and made this decree
Go hunt out the Stone and return it to me

Wi' a too-ra-li-oo-ra-li-oo-ra-li-ay

So the polis went beetlin' away up tae the North
They hunted the Clyde and they hunted the Forth
But the wild folk up yonder just kidded them a'
For they didnae believe it was magic at a'.

Wi' a too-ra-li-oo-ra-li-oo-ra-li-ay

Noo the Provost o' Glesca, Sir Victor by name
Wis awfy put oot when he heard o' the Stane
So he offered the statues that staun in George Square
That the High Church's masons might mak' a few mair.

Wi' a too-ra-li-oo-ra-li-oo-ra-li-ay

When the Dean o' Westminster wi' this was acquaint
He sent for Sir Victor and made him a saint
But it's no good you sending your statues down heah
Said the Dean, But it gives me a jolly good ideah

Wi' a too-ra-li-oo-ra-li-oo-ra-li-ay

So they quarried a stane o' the very same stuff
And they dressed it all up till it looked like enough
Then he sent for the press and announced that the Stane
Had been found and returned tae Westminster again.

Wi' a too-ra-li-oo-ra-li-oo-ra-li-ay

When the reivers found oot what Westminster had done,
They went aboot diggin up stanes by the ton
And fur each wan they quarried they entered the claim
That THIS was the true and original stane.

Wi' a too-ra-li-oo-ra-li-oo-ra-li-ay

But the cream o' the joke still remains tae be telt
For the bloke that wis turnin' them aff on the belt
At the peak o' production was so sorely pressed
That the real yin got bunged in alang wi' the rest

Wi' a too-ra-li-oo-ra-li-oo-ra-li-ay

So if ever ye cam' on a stane wi' a ring
Just sit yersel' doon and proclaim yersel' king
There's nane will be able tae challenge yer claim
That ye've crooned yersel' King on the Destiny Stane

Wi' a too-ra-li-oo-ra-li-oo-ra-li-ay[2]

The four conspirators, now back in Scotland, had the perverse pleasure of speculating with friends and colleagues, the press, the police and others about who might be responsible. Inevitably, in Glasgow a few people were in the know, and a few others stumbled on the truth, but none spoke to the press or the police. Nonetheless, there remained two pressing problems. One was the reaction of King George VI, who was said to be very distressed by the event. At this stage, no one knew whether the Stone of Destiny had been taken by Irish republicans, Scottish nationalists, or indeed by 'ordinary thieves' looking for a ransom. King George was a very popular wartime monarch both in England and in Scotland, and this was an issue which worried many of those who were otherwise supportive. In particular, MacCormick and Gray were concerned about the effect it might have on support for the National Covenant. And so, it

---

2 The reference in the song to the Lord Provost of Glasgow, and the making of copies of the Stone of Destiny alludes to Bailie Robert Gray who had charge of it after its return from London; he had said it would be quite easy to make copies.

was decided to send a petition to the king noting in very formal language and at some length that those who took it were loyal subjects with no thought of treason, that they had no desire to offend His Majesty, but that the Stone of Destiny's rightful resting place was in Scotland. If His Majesty would assure them that the Stone of Destiny would remain in Scotland, it would be returned.

What now to do with this petition? Even though it was still just a few days after the event, a number of prominent people had come out in support of the enterprise, among them was the Earl of Mansfield, the present Earl's grandfather, who was not only a scion of one of the oldest families in Scotland, but also the Lord Lieutenant of Perthshire (i.e. the king's representative in the county), and the Police Convener on Perthshire County Council. *What better source for the petition could there be than Scone Palace?* Ian Hamilton arranged to visit Scone Palace and meet the Earl. The first thing Lord Mansfield said as he entered the room was, 'Let me congratulate you on one of the most brilliant episodes in Scottish history'. While the Earl declined to be the courier for the petition, Hamilton left the meeting in no doubt of his support, and confident that his clandestine visit would remain confidential. Eventually, the petition was left in a Glasgow newspaper office and the media hysteria about the event erupted again.

The other pressing issue was raised by Alan Stuart's father, an engineer. The Stone of Destiny was sandstone, and after 650 years in the Abbey it would be very dry. Now it was in an open field in the middle of a cold, damp and frosty winter. It was in danger of absorbing moisture which would then freeze, and thaw, and might crack it and cause it to crumble. That would be a catastrophe. The Stone of Destiny had to be retrieved as soon as possible.

Consequently, a week after coming back to Scotland, Ian Hamilton set off again for London with Alan Stuart and with Bill Craig, the President of the Glasgow University Union, who had been involved from the beginning, but because of his university duties had not been able to go on the original mission, and John Jocelyn, an Englishman by birth, but a Scottish nationalist by conviction. This time they had Alan Stuart's father's Armstrong-Siddeley, a much bigger and better car, and one with a heater! And they needed it. There was a lot of snow, so much so they had to stop on the way down and buy chains for the rear wheels.

When they neared Rochester, almost exactly 500 miles from Glasgow, they ticked off the landmarks as they approached their destination – to find to their astonishment and dismay two caravans of travelling people parked in the field, with campfires. One of them was right beside the fence on the other side of which lay the Stone of Destiny! Bill Craig, who was an accomplished debater, said he would speak to them. He and Ian Hamilton got out of the car and went to chat to the couple outside the caravan nearest the Stone. It was a long talk, about the weather, and the cold, and the fact that travelling folk are discriminated against, and how in Scotland people are more friendly to them. Craig sympathised with the fact that the establishment was often hostile, and that confrontations with the police were frequent and usually unjustified. When, eventually, they came to the point about the Stone of Destiny, the couple were supportive. However, the man said, 'You can't get it now. There is a local man visiting the other caravan and he is not to be trusted'. After a time, the local man left, and the other couple went to bed, and then the four adventurers manhandled the Stone into the car, and headed north to Scotland.

To put the Stone in the boot would not have been sensible – it would be the first place that the police would examine. Fortunately, they were able to remove the front passenger seat, and the Stone fitted the space well and when covered with a coat was quite inconspicuous. From there the journey north to Glasgow was uneventful by the standards of the previous few days.

The haphazard nature of the operation was never more apparent than when they arrived back in Glasgow for they had not made any plans for the disposal of the Stone of Destiny. Luckily, Bailie Gray came to their rescue once again and took them to Bonnybridge, to a factory owned by a well-known nationalist, John Rollo, who put it in a packing case and hid it in a basement. The next weekend, Ian Hamilton went to Birmingham by train and retrieved the Ford Anglia and brought the smaller section of the Stone back to Scotland. The two pieces of the Stone of Destiny were eventually reunited, and repaired using metal rods by Bailie Gray in a garage in Bearsden.

By the middle of March, Scotland Yard's impatience with the Glasgow police led them to send one of their top detectives and an aide to Scotland. All six student members of the group, Bailie Gray and John MacCormick, and many others as well, were questioned intensively by them. In particular, they homed in on Kay Mathieson, who was by this time, a teacher in Plockton. They interrogated her in Plockton, alone, for five-and-a-half hours, but she gave nothing away.

Once the initial furore had died down a bit, there was the problem of what to do with the Stone of Destiny. As time passed, more and more people became aware of who had been involved in its repatriation and its whereabouts, even though it was moved several times. Although no one talked, this was obviously a risk, and so eventually a decision was made to take it to Arbroath and leave it in the ruins of the Abbey, where the Declaration of Arbroath had been signed by the nobles of Scotland in 1320. This was done at midday on the 11th of April 1951, just a few days after the 631st anniversary of the Declaration. The Stone of Destiny, with a saltire draped over it, was placed next to the site of the High Altar. Accompanying it was a note expressing the hope that the authorities would arrange for its proper display in Scotland. It stated that the location should be decided after consultation with the General Assembly of the Church of Scotland, which as the successor to the Abbots of Scone, and in the absence of a Scottish Parliament, was its rightful guardian.

The peremptory way in which the Stone of Destiny was repossessed by the police later that day generated considerable and widespread anger. It was whisked away without ceremony, deposited in a locked police cell in Forfar, uplifted from there at 1 am the following morning, transported by road to Glasgow and then escorted down to London. The whole operation was totally inept. There had been vague promises from politicians and Church officials that if the Stone of Destiny was returned, consideration would be given to locating it in Scotland. But this did not happen and the lack of any consultation caused much offence in Scotland.

In England, on the other hand, many were scandalised at the time because no charges were brought against the perpetrators. This was because the authorities were concerned about the potential for a trial to be politicised. The Attorney General, Sir Hartley Shawcross, who had been an acclaimed prosecutor at the Nuremberg War Crime trials, said in his statement to the House of Commons:

The clandestine removal of the Stone from Westminster Abbey, and the manifest disregard for the sanctity of the Abbey, were vulgar acts of vandalism which have caused great distress and offence both in England and Scotland. I do not think, however, that the public interest requires criminal proceedings to be taken.

It is noticeable that, in his carefully judged statement, he did not use the words 'steal' or 'theft'. Following Sir Hartley Shawcross, however, there were a number of contributions from MPs, who were not so circumspect in their language, every one of them condemning the action, and several using the word 'theft'. It is noteworthy, considering the very different attitudes to the event in Scotland and England, that not one Scottish MP rose to represent the opinion of the substantial section of the Scottish population which rejoiced as each stage of the story unfolded. Not one of the MPs remarked that the Stone of Destiny was indisputably stolen property; that the length of time it had been in Westminster Abbey did not negate that fact; that Edward III had not fulfilled his promise in 1328 to return it; and that therefore, at the very least, consideration should be given to locating it in Scotland.

There was discussion at the highest political level as to what should happen to the Stone of Destiny, and whether the students should be prosecuted, but it was cloaked in such secrecy that the details were not released until 1996. Sir Hartley Shawcross advising against the prosecution in a paper for the Cabinet wrote:

> I am satisfied that a prosecution would do no good except to the defendants, to whom it would give the opportunity of being regarded as martyrs if they were convicted, or heroes if they were acquitted.

This view was supported by Scotland's Lord Advocate who wrote:

> The prevailing view in Scotland is that those who removed the Stone were foolish rather than criminal, and that it would do no good and might do considerable harm to proceed against them.

Clement Attlee's postwar Labour government was in difficulty. Although it had won the 1950 general election, the large majority that it had achieved in 1945 was down to only five seats, and another election was expected soon. The decision not to prosecute was made in Cabinet on the 19th of April 1951.

So far as the ultimate location of the Stone of Destiny was concerned, the government decided to play a waiting game. In April 1951, Hector McNeil, the Secretary of State for Scotland, submitted a paper outlining three options:

1. Leave the Stone in Westminster.

2. Return to Scotland between coronations.

3. Display it first in Edinburgh and then in various other capitals of the Commonwealth.

Other ministers were unsure, and Attlee himself was opposed, and so no decision was taken. Meanwhile, the Stone of Destiny was stored in the Islip's Chapel in Westminster Abbey and not replaced in the throne.

On the 7th of May 1951, the government decided to postpone a decision for a year, and in particular await the result of a debate on the issue in the General Assembly of the Church of Scotland, due on the 27th of May. The motion before the Assembly came from the Church and Nation committee and proposed that the authorities should 'entrust the guardianship of the Stone to Scottish hands on Scottish soil'.

Ultimately, the General Assembly voted to delete the issue and concentrate on more spiritual matters, and so pressure on the government subsided.

When eventually the general election was held in October 1951, the Conservative Party was returned, but the matter of the Stone of Destiny was not high on its list of immediate priorities. Then following the death of George VI on the 6th of February 1952, the looming coronation ensured that a decision about the Stone of Destiny became urgent. Thus, on the 26th of February 1952, more than a year after the raid on the Abbey, the Stone of Destiny was replaced in the throne in Westminster Abbey without any ceremony and the following brief announcement was made in the House of Commons by Winston Churchill, the new Prime Minister:

> For over 650 years the Stone has been in Westminster Abbey
> and, from its use in successive Coronations it has a historic
> significance for all the countries of the Commonwealth. With
> the approval of Her Majesty's Government, the Stone has been
> restored to its traditional place.

In Scotland, the reaction to the temporary repossession of the Stone of Destiny was an indication of slowly-changing attitudes to self-government. Among the milestones charting this gradual development was the raid on Westminster Abbey on Christmas Day, 1950, and the return of the Stone of Destiny to Scotland more than four and a half decades later in 1996.

Chapter 8
Bailie Gray's Stone and Other Replicas

MOST PEOPLE were satisfied that the stone returned to Westminster Abbey was the one 'clandestinely removed' by the four Glasgow students. But not quite everyone – for there was a persistent rumour that the stone left in Arbroath Abbey was a copy, and that the real one was elsewhere in Scotland, its location known only to a few families who refused to divulge its whereabouts.

Conspicuously, there was at least one well-publicised copy of the Stone of Destiny. This had been made in 1929 by Bailie Robert Gray at his monumental stonemason's yard in Glasgow and had been part of an earlier plot to remove the Stone from Westminster Abbey and substitute it with this copy. However, that plot was discovered and abandoned, but Bailie Gray kept the stone and exhibited it for a time in the window of his premises as publicity for his business, and so it was well-known. Indeed, it was used by Hamilton to see if it would be possible for a couple of young men to move it. In fact, however, it was significantly smaller and lighter than the original.

To add to the uncertainty of the provenance of the stone now in London, Bailie Gray's stone had not been seen and identified since the spring of 1951, and there was no record of what had happened to it.

Furthermore, many believed that at least one other copy had been made by Bailie Gray in the early months of 1951, when the Stone of Destiny was being moved around various locations in Glasgow to avoid detection by the police. It was during that time that the Stone of Destiny was repaired by Bailie Gray and the broken fragment reunited with the main part and secured with brass rods. While he had possession of the Stone of Destiny, it is said that he was able to make another copy of it, and some claimed that this copy was so good that even those who made it were unable to distinguish it from the original. The possibility existed that it was this second copy that was left in Arbroath, and that the original Stone of Destiny remained hidden in Scotland.

Although the evidence indicated that the stone returned to London was without doubt the one uplifted by the Glasgow students, the authorities in London at this time were concerned that its provenance should be confirmed absolutely. In particular, they were worried that doubts about its authenticity would lead to questions about the validity of the forthcoming coronation of Queen Elizabeth. And so they commissioned a study by the Home Office Police Scientific Department, which x-rayed the stone, and confirmed that it had indeed been broken and repaired with metal rods. Almost everyone was satisfied that this was indeed the stone acquired by Edward I.

Nevertheless, the rumours continued and were magnified by the fact that none of the putative copy stones was available for inspection. The only stone on show was the one in London. Then, in 1963, a group which called themselves the Scottish Guardians of the Stone of Destiny claimed that they had possessed the real stone since 1951, and that it had been hidden in Dullatur in Dumbartonshire. They added that its hiding place was about to be redeveloped, and that the Stone of Destiny would have to be moved. But they did not say what was going to happen to it, or put it on display, and nothing was verified.

Nearly ten years later, in 1972, another stone, or perhaps the same stone, and allegedly the 'real' Stone of Destiny, appeared in Parliament Square, in Edinburgh. This time it was taken into custody by the 1320 Club, a nationalist organisation whose president was the poet Hugh MacDiarmid, and whose members included some well-respected nationalists including Wendy Wood, Douglas Young and Frederick Boothby (cousin of Bob Boothby MP). The Club was a cultural and political organisation, but it harboured some with extreme views, and a few of its members were willing to engage in illegal and paramilitary activities in support of their cause. Frederick Boothby, for example, was eventually jailed for complicity in an attempted bank robbery carried out to secure funds for these activities.

The 1320 Club passed the stone to the Reverend John MacKay Nimmo, one of its members, who was a Church of Scotland parish minister, based in St Columba's Church in Lochee in Dundee. The stone was received officially into his church at a service on the 6th of June 1972 (St Columba Day), which was attended by a number of 1320 luminaries including Hugh MacDiarmid, and also by Bailie Gray, who told Nimmo's wife he would not have attended if he thought the stone was a fake. The 1320 Club issued a statement avowing their stone's authenticity: 'We are not ones to play practical jokes on ministers. and would not palm them off with some substitute'.

The stone was put on display in St Columba's Church behind a protective iron grill where it remained for seventeen years. Beside it was a plaque which read:

LIA FÀIL

The Stone of Destiny has been set here, an appropriate place for a symbol so venerable and significant in Scottish history. It has been given into the keeping of the Minister and Kirk Session of St. (Columcille) Columba's Parish Church, Dundee by the 1320 Club in association with Bailie (Municipal Officer and Magistrate) Robert Gray of Glasgow, who helped place the (fake) stone in Arbroath Abbey on 6th April 1951.

The Reverend John MacKay Nimmo was a long-standing nationalist, and friend of Bailie Gray, who along with some other 1320 Club members was a Chevalier of the Knights Templar.

The original Knights Templar was a monastic order founded in the twelfth century in Jerusalem. Unlike other monastic orders which universally espoused peace, non-violence and prayer, the mandate of the Knights Templar was to bear arms in order to protect Christians making a pilgrimage to the Holy Land. In due course, the original Knights Templar fell into desuetude and was disbanded, but several modern organisations claim to be its legitimate successors. The Reverend John MacKay Nimmo was the chaplain to a group of Scottish Templars, the Saint Maol-Rubha Preceptory of the Sovereign and Military Order of the Temple of Jerusalem.[1]

In 1989, St Columba's Church was suddenly found to be unsafe due to dry rot and was closed at very short notice. It was later demolished and replaced by a care home which has some similar external architectural features, and also bears the name 'St Columba'. The stone was passed back to the care of the Knights Templar which some years previously had

1 Saint Maol-Rubha (672–722) was an Irish monk who established a monastery in Applecross and a 'cell' or chapel at Dunstaffnage.

acquired the redundant parish church at Dull near Aberfeldy, and the stone was installed there behind an iron grille.

Dull Church.

In 1990, the Knights Templar passed this stone to Elspeth King, curator of the People's Palace museum in Glasgow, in an effort to have its authenticity confirmed.

The People's Palace consulted Harry Stanger Ltd, a materials testing firm, which examined it and deemed it to be a fake or a copy. The firm reported that there was no sign of the natural flaw in the stone where it had broken when being removed from Westminster Abbey in 1950, nor any evidence of the repairs carried out by Bailie Gray, although there was a chiselled line in the stone obviously made to simulate the flaw.

Subsequently, the Knights Templar sold Dull Church, and the stone was removed into care of Neil MacLeod, at that time the headmaster of Kenmore Primary School, and also a member of the Knights Templar. He and the late Alex Murray (a former Provost of Perth & Kinross), who farmed the land around Dull Church, took possession of the stone and as a temporary measure kept it in a shed near the farm – in fact an ancient cruck shed. It was later moved to another shed which, several years after

The last resting place of Bailie Gray's Stone –
An ancient cruck shed, near Camserney Farm, Dull.

that, was demolished to make way for house building and the stone was lost, A search of the area did not reveal any stones which looked remotely like the Stone of Destiny.

The publicity around the sale of Dull Church by the Knights Templar and the removal of the stone from the church, prompted the Grand Priory of Knights Templar in Scotland to issue the following statement to the *Dundee Courier*:

> There is a group of Scottish Templars who have Bailie Gray's fake Stone of Destiny that used to be in his shop window. Bailie Gray was the stonemason who hid, and repaired, the Westminster stone when it was stolen by Scottish Nationalists in the 1950s. Bailie Gray used the fake in his shop window as a publicity stunt. Once the Westminster Stone was recovered the fake disappeared but re-appeared in Parliament Square in Edinburgh in 1972. The Rev John Nimmo took ownership of the stone until his Dundee Lochee Church closed and then the stone was moved to a Scottish Knights Templar Church at Dull, Aberfeldy. On the sale of this church the fake stone was moved around the country and its current whereabouts are unknown. The Westminster stone was moved to Scotland in

1996 and by Historic Scotland's own admittance, 'The left foot wear on one side of the stone appears to reflect its use as a step in a cylindrical staircase!'. Historians will tell you that the real stone of Scone was probably black in colour. This stone has never been found.

This statement removes any doubt about the provenance of the stone which appeared suddenly in Parliament Square, and was then displayed first in St Columba's Parish Church, Dundee, and latterly in Dull Church, and is now almost certainly lost beside a private road near Aberfeldy. Apart from the 1320 Club and the Knights Templar, no other organisation has ever claimed to have a genuine copy of the Westminster stone, and we now know that the stone that was exhibited in St Columba's Church, Lochee, for so many years was indeed Bailie Gray's copy made in 1929.

There is a minor postscript to this story. Highland Safaris, a company which organise Land Rover safaris on the moorland above Loch Tay, and owned much of the land in that area, commissioned another copy stone which was placed on two short pillars, similar to those used in Scone Palace and sited on the moorland beside the Camserney Burn. This, they told their clientele, was the 'real Stone of Destiny'. Sadly, although the stone pillars remain, the stone itself has also disappeared.

The Arlington Stone

There are at least three other 'Stones of Destiny', one of which claims to be the original stone. It is in *The Arlington Bar*, in Woodlands Road, Glasgow, one of the longest-established pubs in the city. The story, according to the staff at *The Arlington*, is that the four students, 'after a 500-mile journey back home to Scotland in a Ford Anglia hoisted the Stone of Destiny on to the bar top of *The Arlington*, and celebrated their new acquisition with a pint'. Thereafter, the Stone of Destiny was hidden in the pub in a box seat for more than 50 years until the bar was refurbished in 2007 and the new owner put it on display. Above the stone is a notice explaining how it happened:

* * *

The Arlington Stone in a niche in the wall of The Arlington Bar.

From the 13th Century
Kings and Queens have been crowned on
THE STONE OF DESTINY

Seven centuries after Edward Longshanks marched triumphantly out of Scotland with the ancient symbol of Caledonian nationhood effectively tucked under his arm, the Stone of Destiny crossed the border again in 1996 receiving an emotional homecoming in Edinburgh, after being held at Westminster Abbey for seven centuries.

The Stone however already came back in 1950. Daring students from Glasgow University stole it from Westminster Abbey on Christmas morning! Roadblocks were set up yet the Stone still made it north to Glasgow. For a respite these thirsty students carried it from their car and placed it on the bar of 'The Arlington' whilst enjoying a pint.

Within two weeks the game was up and the police were tipped off that the Stone could be found at 'The Arlington'. Under pressure the students decided to hand it back. Or did they? Stories abound across Scotland that the students handed a replica to the police and that the 'real' Stone is here at 'The Arlington Bar'.

While it is a good story, and undoubtedly a marketing gimmick, it is far from credible. Although the stone has rings and chains attached to staples in its end, it does not have the grooves cut in the top surface. Moreover its general shape is oval rather than square – more like a pillow than a building block. At 740 x 420 x 231 mm, it is a little longer and thinner than the real Stone.

Scone Palace Stone

There are two other replicas of the Stone of Destiny, but no wild claims about their origin. The Scone Palace stone was commissioned in 1984 by the Earl of Mansfield to enhance the attraction of Scone Palace as a visitor destination. It is approximately the same size as the one in the museum (681 x 390 x 292 mm), but is not a good copy. In particular, it does not have any grooves cut in the top face, and while it does have iron staples and rings, these are inserted into the top of the stone rather than the ends, and there are no figure of eight links. It is mounted on two short pillars and displayed on Moot Hill outside the Mansfield Mausoleum in front of Scone Palace. Situated now as near as it is possible to be to the place, outside the Abbey church, where the monarchs of Scotland were crowned, it emphasises the importance of Moot Hill in mediaeval Scotland.

Replica of the Scone Palace Stone on Moot Hill, Scone Palace.

The Scone Palace stone is surrounded by paving slabs, nine of which are engraved with the names of Scots monarchs who are said (in the accompanying notice) to have been inaugurated on the real Stone of

Destiny at Scone. The list includes Robert the Bruce, about whose ceremony there is some doubt, as discussed earlier, and Charles II, who would have sat on the Stone of Destiny when he was crowned in Westminster Abbey as King of England in 1660, but definitely not when he was inaugurated in Scone as King of Scots, eleven years earlier in 1649.

Arbroath Abbey Stone

There is yet another replica of the Stone of Destiny, which is on view at the visitor centre at Arbroath Abbey. It was made as a prop to be used in the pageants that were staged to celebrate the signing of the Declaration of Arbroath in 1320. These took place eighteen times between 1947 and 2005, and it is hoped they will resume in the future.

The Arbroath Abbey Stone.

It is smaller than the real stone at 640 mm x 280 mm x 240 mm and lacks the chiselled grooves and pits on the top surface. Instead of staples and figure of eight links, solid iron bars have been bolted to the end faces. It was obviously not intended to be examined closely.

Chapter 9
Pressure Mounts to Return the Stone to Scotland

FOLLOWING THE END of the First Scottish War of Independence in 1328, the Stone of Destiny remained in its throne in Westminster Abbey until 1950. In the late-nineteenth and early-twentieth centuries, it was accorded major cultural significance, especially by the British State. It was invested with powerful symbolism representing the constancy and permanence of the (unwritten) constitution and the organs of the British (English) State – monarchy, Parliament and the Anglican Church. Furthermore, perhaps because of its perceived origin in Egypt, and Biblical associations, it was considered to be a binding agent in the cohesion of the Empire and later the Commonwealth, although why this should be seems, from a twenty-first-century perspective, to be something of a mystery.

These beliefs went into overdrive during the first half of the last century. Spencer Acklom, writing during the First World War, claimed that it was, 'the stone Pillar of our national identification', and another, Adam Rutherford, in 1937, described it as, 'the most important, the most wonderful, the most sublime stone in the world'.

During the Second World War, F T Perry wrote that the Stone of Destiny, 'was the magnet of the Empire binding all its people in one…the foundation stone of an empire'. There were also the most remarkable religious attributes ascribed to the Stone of Destiny. Adam Rutherford asserted that, 'The present place of the Stone of Israel in the Coronation Chair of the greatest empire the world has ever known, beautifully symbolises Christ in His office of King of Kings and Lord of Lords'.

This cultural importance of the Stone of Destiny was well understood by the suffragettes who on the evening of the 12th of June 1914, exploded a bomb, loaded with nuts and bolts, behind the Coronation Chair. The explosion was timed perfectly to take place just when MPs in the House of Commons nearby were debating how to cope with the increasingly violent methods of the militant suffragettes. The bomb caused considerable damage to the back of the ancient oak chair and parts of it were broken away completely; it was, however, repaired in due course.

Although there was no apparent damage to the Stone of Destiny itself, it may have been that the explosion loosened the natural flaw in the stone, causing it to split when Hamilton and his colleagues bumped it out of the Coronation Chair during their raid on the Abbey in 1950. Meanwhile, the suffragettes had made their point, but there were no arrests and the perpetrators were never identified.

The importance of the Stone of Destiny, as perceived by the establishment of the Church and State in England was also underlined by the measures taken to protect it during both world wars. In 1915, the Coronation Chair and the Stone of Destiny were moved to the crypt under the Chapter House for protection from bombing raids. Then, again, in late 1939, as the storm clouds of war gathered and the threat of much heavier enemy bombardment and ultimately invasion mounted, the throne was moved to Gloucester Cathedral, while the Stone of Destiny was secretly buried beneath the Islip Chapel in Westminster Abbey, lest Britain and its government should fall to the Nazis. Its location was disclosed only to the Marquess of Willingdon, the Governor General of Canada, who was safely out of harm's way in Ottawa. There was to be no possibility of Adolf Hitler following Oliver Cromwell as a usurper of the British monarchy, and sitting on the Stone of Destiny! Even in 1950, these attitudes were still strong and explain the overreaction of the Church and State to the raid by the Glasgow students.

Attempts to Repossess the Stone

In the last quarter of the nineteenth century, the independence movement in Ireland was gathering strength, and there was renewed interest in the cultural icons of the Irish people, and especially in the Stone of Destiny and the Lia Fàil, although the two were often confused. And so, the first illicit effort to seize the Stone of Destiny came not from Scottish nationalists, but from an Irish cultural and nationalist organisation named Clan na Gael which was based in America. It consisted of descendants of Irish immigrants to the USA, many of whose families had fled their country in the aftermath of the Great Hunger (*An Gorta Mòr*) of the late 1840s and early 1850s, and it included in its ranks many who later became prominent in the Irish-American establishment. By the 1880s, it had also attracted a militant faction (the Dynamite Men) who were implicated in gun running into England from America. In 1884, an elaborate plan was hatched, whereby a group of men inside the Abbey would disarm the police, and then pass the Stone of Destiny through a window to others waiting outside, who were to take it away to Ireland.

Their organisation had, however, been penetrated by the British spy, Thomas Miller Beach (known in the USA and Ireland as Major Henri le Caron) who had risen to a high rank in the American wing of the organisation. The attempt to seize the Stone was eventually aborted. and the ringleaders of the plot were able to slip away back to the US without being apprehended.[1]

In Scotland, on the other hand, in the first half of the twentieth century, the perception of a shared British identity was at its peak – due no doubt to the success of the Empire in which Scots people played such a prominent and successful role, and the absence of the brutal military suppression that had been experienced in Ireland. Neil Munro, writing towards the end of the First World War, has Para Handy, the captain of the Clyde puffer, *Vital Spark*, refer to himself approvingly as, 'One of Brutain's (*sic*) hardy sons', which encapsulates the Unionist sentiments which were fairly universal at that time in 'North Britain'. Politically, this was manifest in the results of the postwar general elections, and reached its zenith in 1955, when the Conservatives won an overall majority of seats in Scotland – the only time that this has happened.[2] Nevertheless, there was a growing resentment at the dominance of London, and the attention devoted to Ireland.

The First Irish Home Rule Bill was introduced in the House of Commons in 1886 but was defeated after a split in the Liberal Party. The second bill in 1893 was defeated in the House of Lords, but the third, introduced in 1912, after the Lord's veto was removed, was enacted in 1914, but suspended due to the outbreak of the First World War, and not enacted after the war. In regard to Home Rule, Scotland lagged behind Ireland, although the Stone of Destiny did not feature in any of the Home Rule Bills.

---

1 Major Henri le Caron (aka Thomas Miller Beach), *Twenty-Five Years in the Secret Service: The Recollections of a Spy* (Wentworth Press, 2016).

2 In Scotland the 'Conservatives' consisted of an alliance between the Unionist Party (Scotland), which was the dominant right-wing party in Scotland, the National Liberal Party, and the Conservative Party.

William Cowan, MP for Kirkcaldy, introduce the Government of Scotland Bill in May 1913, which passed its second reading by 204 votes to 159. This would have created a very strong parliament in Scotland, with powers 'over all Scottish affairs' including matters that are not devolved even yet, such as pensions and national insurance. Because of the outbreak of war, it was never enacted. An attempt to reintroduce it in 1924 was 'talked out' by the Conservative opposition, causing such an uproar in the House of Commons that David Kirkwood, the Labour MP for Dumbarton Burghs, was suspended from the House. Following this defeat, Kirkwood introduced a Private Member's Bill seeking the return of the Stone to Scotland. It passed the first reading by 201 voters to 171, but was not allowed sufficient time by the government to complete its stages, 'owing to the pressure of other business', and so it fell. The same fate overtook another attempt to reintroduce the Government of Scotland Bill in 1926.

Although there were no further Parliamentary attempts to return the Stone of Destiny to Scotland, the matter was raised in Parliamentary questions. In the House of Lords, in 1952, Arthur George Murray, the third Viscount Elibank (near Selkirk) asked the government if they would consider restoring the Stone of Destiny to Scotland following the coronation which was due in 1953. Predictably, the request was refused. Some months later – after the coronation – Emrys Hughes, a Welshman, but Labour MP for South Ayrshire for many years, raised the matter in the House of Commons.[3] He is quoted in *Hansard*:

> Is the Prime Minister aware that it costs a great deal to keep this Stone in Westminster Abbey, and that there are special installations which, whenever a Scotsman approaches the Stone, ring a bell in Scotland Yard?

Winston Churchill, the Prime Minister at the time, did not contradict this unlikely situation, but merely responded, 'I do not think it is worthwhile to grudge the small expense to maintain this historic continuity'.

In 1967, and again in 1973 and 1974, as nationalist aspirations increased in Scotland and were accompanied by electoral success for the SNP, there

---

3 Hughes had strong links to Ayrshire. He married Nan Hardie, the daughter of Keir Hardie in 1924, both serving as councillors (and Provosts) on Cumnock Council (South Ayrshire).

were three further illicit attempts to retrieve the Stone of Destiny for Scotland. They were all perpetrated by single individuals and were even more amateurish than the raid in 1950, and all failed miserably. On the 14th of June 1967, John Patrick O'Byrne, a 25-year-old Scot, successfully secreted himself in the Abbey. Unfortunately, when he tried to lift the Stone of Destiny from its place in the Coronation Chair, he found it was too heavy for him to move. Nevertheless, he set off the alarm, which did not sound in the Abbey but in New Scotland Yard, and, it is said, in two neighbouring police stations. The unfortunate O'Byrne was apprehended as he left the Abbey. He was charged with breaking and entering the Abbey with intent to steal the Stone of Destiny, and fined £7 10/–, and put on probation.

In 1973, there was another illicit attempt to repatriate the Stone of Destiny which only came to light when the official files were released in 1996. A Glasgow student, who is unnamed, made an attempt to remove it, which was quickly discovered, and he was apprehended, though never charged.

A more serious attempt to repatriate the Stone of Destiny was made by David Carmichael Stewart on the 4th of September 1974, and was again thwarted by failure to appreciate the weight of the stone. Stewart had made a large canvas sling with which he intended to swing the Stone of Destiny from the Coronation Chair, and then lower it onto a trolley which he had built at home. He had also constructed a ramp to be used to haul the Stone of Destiny into his Mini car (the original version of the 'Mini', not a modern BMW Mini!) Remarkably, he managed to take all this equipment, including the trolley, which he had dismantled, into the Abbey without being detected. He then hid under the altar until the nightwatchman had done his rounds, and proceeded to extract the Stone of Destiny. Unfortunately, one of the iron railings which he was using to secure his sling broke, the Stone of Destiny slipped and crashed down crushing his trolley, and setting off the alarm. He had no alternative but to abandon the project and try to make his escape.

Like John Patrick O'Byrne, he was apprehended by the police as he was trying to make his getaway from the Abbey. He was charged with attempted theft, and spent the next week in Brixton Prison. Stewart, however, was fortunate that his attempt took place between the April and October 1974 general elections. The SNP had won an historic seven seats in the April election, and were on course to do even better in October, which in due course they did, winning eleven seats. Stewart made it clear that his defence would be to contest the ownership of the Stone of Destiny and testify that he was seeking to return stolen property. The government was unhappy about contesting the matter of stolen property and unwilling to risk making any political martyrs, and so the charge of theft was dropped. Shortly after the October general election, Stewart appeared before Bow Street Magistrates Court, was conditionally discharged and ordered to pay £150 of damages and £75 costs.

Due to pressure on newspaper editors from the government, none of these episodes achieved the prominence in the press that they would otherwise have done, and indeed deserved.

———————————

Chapter 10
The Stone Returns to Scotland –
St Andrew's Day, 1996

THE FOLLOWING Parliamentary Statement and exchanges, quoted from *Hansard*, occurred in the House of Commons on the 3rd of July 1996, immediately following Questions to the Secretary of State for Scotland. It was a noisy session:

> **Madam Speaker (Miss Betty Boothroyd):** I call the Prime Minister.

> **The Prime Minister (Mr John Major):** With permission, Madam Speaker, I should like to make a statement about the Stone of Destiny. The Stone of Destiny is the most ancient symbol of Scottish kingship. It was used in the coronation of Scottish Kings until the end of the 13th century. Exactly 700 years ago, in 1296, King Edward I brought it from Scotland and housed it in Westminster Abbey. It remains—[Interruption].

> **Madam Speaker:** Order. The House must come to order and hear this statement in good order. There will be Hon. Members who will want to be called after the statement. They should listen to it now.

> **The Prime Minister:** The stone remains the property of the Crown. I wish to inform the House that, on the advice of Her Majesty's Ministers, the Queen has agreed that the stone should be returned to Scotland. The stone will, of course, be taken to Westminster Abbey to play its traditional role in the coronation ceremonies of future sovereigns of the United Kingdom.

> The Stone of Destiny holds a special place in the hearts of Scots. On this the 700th anniversary of its removal from Scotland, it is appropriate to return it to its historic homeland. I am sure that the House would wish to be assured that the stone will be placed in an appropriate setting in Scotland. The

Government will be consulting Scottish and Church opinion about that. The stone might be displayed in Edinburgh castle alongside the Honours of Scotland, Europe's oldest crown jewels. Alternatively, it might be appropriate to place it in St. Margaret's chapel inside the castle or in St. Giles's cathedral. There may be other options.

Once these consultations have been completed, the necessary arrangements will be made, and the Stone will be installed with due dignity.

The news that the Stone of Destiny was to be returned to Scotland came as a considerable surprise to practically everyone, north and south of the border. While most Scots, not just political and cultural nationalists, agreed that it was right and proper that the Stone of Destiny should come back to Scotland, that objective was not high on anyone's list of priorities. The 700th anniversary of Edward I's acquirement of the Stone of Destiny fell on the 8th of August 1996, but there had been no proposals for any recognition of the date, and certainly no agitation for its return. Those who did advocate devolution or independence were far more interested in the political, economic and social outcomes, rather than the return of an historic symbol that was, by this time, considered almost irrelevant in the modern era, except as a tourist attraction. There were, nevertheless, a number of small cultural groups, which did agitate for its return. Of these, that led by Robbie the Pict (see Chapter 12) was perhaps the most prominent. Robbie pursued the matter relentlessly but this campaign fell on deaf ears in officialdom, and it had no significant effect on the public mood nor on any of the political parties, none of which had ever referred to the Stone of Destiny in any of their manifestos.

The reaction in England was different, once again, from that in Scotland, and was generally hostile. Comments from the Dean and Chapter of Westminster Abbey, and other members of the Anglican establishment were remarkably similar to those which were voiced following the raid on the Abbey in 1950, although they were less strident, and emphasised more the sacramental and religious associations of the Stone of Destiny. Much of the London-based press, however, was less restrained. The *London Evening Standard* called the proposal, 'an act of indefensible vandalism', and the *Spectator* criticised John Major's 'false and throwaway approach' to such an important symbol of the Union.

In the House of Commons, however, the leader of the Labour Party, Tony Blair, and Sir David Steele, for the Liberal Democrats, were supportive, as were almost all those who contributed to the debate. Many backbench MPs on the other hand, especially on the Labour side, considered the matter to be irrelevant, and this led to some cynical flippancy, which was condemned by Madam Speaker. John Maxton, the Labour MP for Cathcart, articulated the views of the Labour leadership in Scotland in a short but measured contribution during which he said that he believed that the return of a 'feudal, mediaeval symbol of tyranny' was not important when what Scotland really needed at this time, was the establishment of a modern democratic parliament. Margaret Ewing, for the SNP, while also supporting the return of the Stone of Destiny, pointed out that it was not, as the Prime Minister had stated, a symbol of Scottish kingship, but the symbol of the sovereignty of the people of Scotland, which had been enunciated through the Declaration of Arbroath.

Outside of the debating chamber of the House of Commons, many politicians and newspaper columnists considered the proposal to be an ill-conceived and patronising party-political move by the Prime Minister and Michael Forsyth, the Secretary of State for Scotland to try to bolster the Conservative Party's flagging fortunes in Scotland. Back in Scotland, the main issue was where the Stone of Destiny should be displayed. Perth was keen to have it, but there was no obvious place to put it. Scone Palace was a private house which is closed to visitors during the winter. St John's Kirk was not keen to shoulder the responsibility of looking after it, and the then Perth Museum & Art Gallery was too small. Stirling could have had it in the castle, but eventually the decision was taken to install it in Edinburgh.

Why did it happen? What were the factors that influenced Michael Forsyth, the Conservative MP for Stirling, and Secretary of State for Scotland, to propose the Stone of Destiny's return, and the Prime Minister to agree?

John Major relates in his memoirs that his reaction to Michael Forsyth's proposal was initially non-committal, but that events gradually began to make the return look more attractive. *Was this change of view influenced by the published opinion polls and bye-election results?* The nationalist voice at Westminster had been weak, indeed feeble, since its nadir at the general election in 1979, when the SNP vote collapsed and lost nine of the eleven seats it had gained in 1974. Although there had been a slight improvement to three MPs in the general election of 1983, and this was maintained in 1987 and 1992, superficially the political threat from the SNP seemed to be dead in the water. Nonetheless, those who looked deeper into the figures, and in particular at the level of support for the SNP (as opposed to the number of MPs elected), and the breadth of its vote across the country, could see signs of the SNP's growth and electoral potential.

Forsyth was a man whose political antennae were acutely sensitive, and he was certainly one of those who could read the runes. He claims that he had considered that the Stone of Destiny should be returned to Scotland ever since his childhood, but it is hard to believe that the political events developing as his party approached the 1997 general election were not a major influence. In the 1992 general election, the SNP vote had increased by 50 per cent, though this was not translated into an increase in the number of seats won. Then in the 1994 regional elections, the SNP made significant gains, and these were consolidated at the new Unitary Local Authority elections in 1995. Later in 1995, following the death of Sir Nicholas Fairbairn, the SNP won the quintessentially Tory constituency of Perth & North Perthshire in a bitterly fought bye-election.

In fact, Forsyth's concern was well-founded. Indeed, it may have been a premonition. A year and a half after the Perth and North Perthshire bye-election, in the general election of 1997, the Conservative Party lost all of its eleven Scottish constituencies, including Forsyth's Stirling seat. The main beneficiary, however, was not the SNP, but the Scottish Labour Party which increased its tally of Scottish MPs to 56. Meanwhile, the SNP moved up to six MPs although its vote increased only marginally, and the Liberal Democrats gained one seat to return ten MPs. It is difficult to believe that the return of the Stone of Destiny to Scotland had made any political impact at all. However, it did have an impact on Michael Forsyth who was knighted after his general election defeat, and he incorporated an image of the Stone of Destiny into his coat of arms. Two years later, he was raised to the Peerage as Baron Forsyth of Drumlean.

* * *

The actual return of the Stone of Destiny to Edinburgh was an opportunity to lay on an elaborate display of pomp and circumstance, requiring a great deal of military precision and meticulous timing. It involved careful planning and employed several elements of the military, and much cross-border collaboration.

The Stone of Destiny began its journey from Westminster Abbey to Scotland on the 13th of November 1996. The plans were top secret and conceived with security as the main consideration. A special scaffold, with a block and tackle, had been designed and constructed to ease the stone from out of its housing beneath the throne, and lower it onto a specially-made handbarrow, where it was carefully packed to protect it during its forthcoming journey home. The whole operation took over six hours and it was then left, fully guarded, in the Abbey overnight. It is interesting to compare this elaborate operation with what happened the previous time that the Stone of Destiny left Westminster Abbey. The next morning, before daybreak, it was carried from Westminster Abbey by security guards, accompanied by the Dean, the Very Reverend Michael Mann, and placed in a police Land Rover. Then, accompanied by an Army escort, it was driven north to Ablemarle Barracks in Northumberland, where it rested overnight, still under an armed guard.

Early on the 15th of November, after some delay due to a hoax bomb scare, it continued north in a convoy of two Land Rovers, a white minibus, and an escort from the Coldstream Guards. The destination was the mid-point of the bridge over the River Tweed at Coldstream, the border between England and Scotland, where it arrived at five minutes past eleven o'clock. This point on the border was chosen because the bridge carries what was the most important of the major historic routes between England and Scotland, now the A697. There, a reception party awaited to welcome the Stone of Destiny back into Scotland after 700 years of exile. It was led by the Lord Lieutenant of Berwickshire, and included the Secretary of State for Scotland, Michael Forsyth, representatives of the main political parties in Scotland, and a new escort drawn from the Royal Scots and the Kings Own Scottish Borderers. A combined military brass and pipe band played a specially commissioned quick march, 'The Return of the Stone', as the procession made its way to the former Town House of Coldstream. More formalities followed and Forsyth made a speech during which he said:

> I learned about the Stone of Destiny when I was seven years old, and I always believed that it should be in Scotland. There is no political agenda here at all. Its return is not going to make a huge difference, but it is an important part of our heritage.

Despite the publicity surrounding the occasion, there was only a small crowd of onlookers, many of whom were disappointed that the Stone of Destiny was not actually on view.

Following the ceremonies at Coldstream, the Stone of Destiny was taken to Edinburgh where its protective packaging was removed at Historic Scotland's Conservation Centre at South Gyle, enabling it to be examined professionally for the first time by specialists in Scotland. First of all, it was cleaned and then photographed by Historic Scotland's senior photographer, David Henrie, and drawings were made by the artist Ian Scott. It was also taken to the National Museum of Scotland where it was x-rayed again using the most modern equipment. These images confirmed the line of the break in the Stone of Destiny and its repair using three, probably solid, metal rods. It was during this period that it was examined in detail by Peter Hill (see Chapter 12).

'Mystery Message Found in Stone' – Headline in The Sun, Friday, the 13th of December 1996

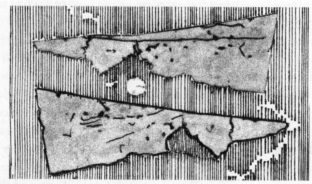

The two sides of the slip of paper which was discovered in a tiny lead tube which had been inserted into the back of the Stone of Destiny.

One of Historic Scotland's more surprising findings was a small dark red blob of sealing wax on the back surface of the stone. The red mark had been noted before, but it was thought that it was an inclusion or pebble embedded in the sandstone. Surprisingly, when the Stone of Destiny arrived at South Gyle, as it was being cleaned with damp swabs, it was discovered that the 'inclusion' was in fact red sealing wax which plugged the end of a tiny lead tube inserted into a hole drilled with a 1/4-inch bit. Inside the tube was a tightly-rolled triangular slip of white paper (95 mm by 33 mm in size). It appears to have been hastily cut from a larger piece of paper which itself had been cut, possibly from a notebook. There was no watermark and nothing was printed on it – no heading, coat of arms, or identifying logo – just some writing with a black ball point pen which had deteriorated so significantly that it was hardly legible, although it was considered that it could have been the signature of S R Andrews, who was the Clerk of Works at Westminster Abbey from 1963 to 1981.

The explanation offered by Westminster Abbey in 1996 was that after Patrick O'Byrne's attempt to retrieve the Stone of Destiny in 1967 there was considerable English concern about the Stone being repossessed by Scottish patriots and there were calls for much greater security for it. These were renewed following the 1974 attempt by David Stewart, and led to the decision by Peter Foster, the Abbey's Surveyor of the Fabric, to 'tag' it. This was to be done by inserting into the Stone of Destiny a slip of paper cut from a larger document which was to be kept in the Abbey. If the occasion arose, the two pieces of paper could be matched, and so confirm the identity of the real stone with certainty. Although this action by the Abbey's surveyor was not recorded anywhere and the original document from which the slip was cut has never been produced, Foster remembered the occasion, and it is the only plausible explanation. Furthermore, it is certain that the message was not the one that some believed had been secreted by Bailie Gray.

Celebrating the Return of the Stone

Although the actual return of the Stone of Destiny to Scotland on the 15th of November was deeply symbolic, the main ceremony was reserved for the transfer of the responsibility for the care and security of it to the Commissioners of the Scottish Regalia representing, allegedly, the people of Scotland. This took place in Edinburgh on the 30th of November, St Andrew's Day, 1996, in the 700th year since its removal from Scotland.

There was no precedent for such an occasion, and so it was modelled on the welcome that might be given to an important visiting Head of State. It involved a remarkable array of the 'Great and the Good' of Scotland, many with heraldic titles (which most modern Scots would not recognise), dressed in colourful period uniforms and fancy hats, parading up the Royal Mile from Holyrood House to a formal service in St Giles Cathedral, and then on to Edinburgh Castle. It was the most spectacular day of pageantry seen in Scotland since the visit to Edinburgh by Her Majesty the Queen following her coronation in 1953. Its pomp and circumstance were copied in many respects at the late Queen Elizabeth's funeral in 2022 and at the coronation of Charles III.

St Andrew's Day in 1996 dawned bright and sunny, but cold. The Stone of Destiny which had been moved to Holyrood Palace was placed in a Perspex topped Land Rover – the 'stone-mobile' – to ensure it was visible to all, but protected from the elements. A fleet of eight limousines carrying the most important guests, accompanied the stone-mobile in the parade up the Royal Mile behind a mounted escort drawn from the Lothian and Borders Police, and the Royal Scots Dragoon Guards. The band of the Royal Marines led the parade playing the theme tune of 'Mission Impossible' – hardly the most appropriate choice of music. The route was lined by soldiers in full-dress uniform. A crowd estimated at 10,000, which was less than expected, turned out to watch.

The names and titles of the principal guests read like lists of the attendants at a coronation. HRH Prince Andrew, the Duke of York, represented HM the Queen. An escort provided by the officers of the Royal Company of Archers, the Queen's Bodyguard in Scotland, wearing their distinctive uniforms and feathered hats, each carrying a longbow and a quiver of arrows, walked on either side of the stone-mobile as it made its way up the Royal Mile. Accompanying Prince Andrew were the four Commissioners of the Regalia, who are, *ex-officio*, the Keeper of the Great Seal of Scotland (the Secretary of State for Scotland), the Lord Justice Clerk, the Lord Advocate, and the Lord Clerk Register. They were followed by the Court of the Lord Lyon King of Arms, consisting of the Lord Lyon himself, the Kintyre Pursuivant, the Carrick Pursuivant, the *Ross Herald*, the *Rothesay Herald*, and the *Albany Herald*, all clad in elaborate colourful tabards. Then came the Lord High Constable of

Scotland (the Earl of Erroll), Gold Stick for Scotland (the Colonel of The Scots Guards), the Hereditary Bearer of the National Banner of Scotland (the Earl of Dundee), and the Hereditary Bearer of the National Flag of Scotland (the Earl of Lauderdale). They made quite a spectacle.

Meanwhile, outside St Giles Cathedral (which is not really a cathedral at all, not having a bishop), the Ecclesiastical Procession led by the Moderator of the General Assembly of the Church of Scotland and the leaders of the other faiths in Scotland waited. With the usual meticulous timing the Stone of Destiny arrived outside the cathedral at 11 am precisely, and was lifted from the Land Rover by bearers provided by the 1st Battalion of the Kings Own Scottish Borderers, and carried into the east end of the Cathedral. Meanwhile, at the west door, a new Guard of Honour formed up, consisting of the 1st Battalion of the Argyll and Sutherland Highlanders and the Highland Band of the Scottish Division, and it was inspected by Prince Andrew.

Then the Moderator entered St Giles Cathedral with the ecclesiastical procession followed by Prince Andrew and the Royal Procession. When Prince Andrew took his place in the Royal Pew, the Stone of Destiny, still escorted by the Royal Company of Archers, was carried in and placed in the sanctuary.

This was to be a National Service celebrating the occasion of the return of the Stone of Destiny to Scotland, and the large congregation was drawn from all walks and all ages of Scottish life. The service was led by the minister of St Giles, the Reverend Gilleasbuig MacMillan, and included ten readings performed by young people from all over Scotland. The Biblical story of the mythical origin of the stone as Jacob's Pillow (Genesis 28, verses 10–22), was read in Gaelic, and the account in the New Testament of the call by Jesus to Andrew on the shore of the Sea of Galilee to become the first of the twelve disciples (John 1, verses 35–42) was read in Doric. The address was given by the Moderator of the General Assembly, the Right Reverend John McIndoe, during which he navigated a difficult path between competing political philosophies, when he said:

> ...during all the long pilgrimage of the years, the ideal of Scottish nationhood and the reality of Scottish identity have never been wholly obliterated from the hearts of the people.

The recovery of this ancient symbol of the Stone cannot but strengthen the proud distinctiveness of the people of Scotland. It will in addition, be a silent and steady witness to the mutuality of interest between those who govern, and those who are governed, united in the task of promoting the welfare of the land and the destination of its people.

After the service, the parade reformed outside St Giles, and the Stone of Destiny was replaced in the stone-mobile for the last leg of its long journey from Westminster Abbey to Edinburgh Castle. It was accompanied for this part of its journey by the Highland Band of the Scottish Division. The bearers carried the Stone of Destiny onto a red-carpeted stage in the centre of the Great Hall of the castle, where it was laid on a raised wooden dais. The Lord Lyon then read the Royal Warrant from Her Majesty the Queen, which legitimised the formal transfer of the responsibility for the Stone of Destiny to the Keepers of the Scottish Regalia. He then passed the Warrant to Prince Andrew who made a short speech, before handing it on to Michael Forsyth, representing the Keepers of the Regalia. Forsyth then made another speech which concluded with the following statement of the political objective of the whole operation:

We are grateful to Her Majesty the Queen for graciously approving the return of the Stone to its ancient homeland, where it will continue to be a powerful reminder of Scotland's heritage and a symbol of the continuity of a nation within the United Kingdom.

At this point a fly-past by typhoon jets roared over the city, and a 21-gun salute was fired from the battery of Edinburgh Castle, and returned from HMS *Newcastle*, anchored in the Port of Leith.

Later that day the Stone of Destiny was moved from the Great Hall and placed adjacent to the Honours of Scotland, the Crown, the Sceptre and the Sword of State in the castle's Crown Room where it has been seen by many hundreds of thousands of people, over the last quarter of a century.

The most recent events involving the Stone of Destiny are, of course, the coronation of King Charles III in London, and then the service in St Giles Cathedral in Edinburgh on the 5th of July 2023. Shortly after the death of the late Queen Elizabeth, the Stone was transported back from Edinburgh Castle to London, without any pomp or ceremony, and installed in the throne in Westminster Abbey to await the coronation. During the actual ceremony, however, the Stone could not be seen, was not referred to by the Archbishop of Canterbury who conducted the actual coronation and was mentioned only very briefly by those who provided the commentary for the enormous TV audience.

Following the coronation in London, the Stone was transported back to Scotland, again without any ceremony, to await the service in St Giles Cathedral. At this service, the new king was presented with the Honours of Scotland – the Elizabeth Sword, the Sceptre and the Crown. On receiving the Sword, Charles accepted the loyalty of the people and promised to defend the law. When presented with the Sceptre, he promised to seek the prosperity of the nation. And at the culmination of the ceremony, with his hand touching the Crown, he promised, 'By God's help', to serve all of his people.

During these procedures, the Stone rested on a plinth in the sanctuary, in full view of the congregation – not hidden under a throne or behind rich embroidered cloths, and it was certainly noted by those providing the TV commentary. Then towards the end of the service, the Lord Lyon stepped forward to draw attention to the presence of the Stone, which was, he declared, an ancient symbol of Scottish sovereignty. 'Carved from the earth', he said, 'this is a simple piece of stone. Yet, in its simplicity, it has precious and significant symbolism for the people of this land'. It emphasised the connection between the land of Scotland and its people. This was the first time the Stone has ever been referred to during a coronation. It was an historic moment in the life of Scotland.

Chapter 11
Homecoming to Perth for the Stone of Destiny

PERTH HAS LONG coveted the Stone of Destiny. To be sure, it really belongs to Scone, but the Abbey where it was kept was destroyed during the Scottish Reformation in 1559 and its stones used and reused in the building of Scone Palace, to the extent that there is now nothing to be seen of the mediaeval Abbey church or the monastic buildings above ground. Moreover, the old Royal Burgh of Scone has also ceased to exist. Its houses were destroyed and its 1,400 souls along with their animals were moved 2 miles east to a new location, which became the village of New Scone at the time when the palace was rebuilt in 1812. All that remains of the Royal Burgh now is the arched gateway which separated the burgh from the palace, the old mercat cross and the graveyard.

Although there were discussions in Parliament about returning the Stone of Destiny to Scotland following the raid on Westminster Abbey in 1950, there was little enthusiasm for the idea even in Scotland. By 1996, however, public opinion in Scotland was changing, and although not enthusiastic, certainly favoured the return of the Stone of Destiny to Scotland. Following Michael Forsyth's intervention, the Cabinet did consider a number of sites where it could be appropriately and securely displayed with year-round free public access assured. Among these were Stirling Castle, Arbroath Abbey, Dunfermline Abbey, the National Museum of Scotland (Edinburgh) and Perth. Security, and sufficient available space to mount an impressive display of the Stone of Destiny, however, were insurmountable problems for the Perth sites, and in due course the Crown Room of Edinburgh Castle was chosen despite its inadequacies. Edinburgh Castle attracts many thousands of visitors every year, and a large proportion of them filed past the exhibition of the Stone of Destiny and the Honours of Scotland, but the site was very restricted and the standard of the display was poor.

By 2009, Perth had begun to appreciate the potential advantages in terms of civic prestige and tourism that the Stone of Destiny would bring, and it began a serious campaign to have it returned as nearly as possible to its original home in Scone. That year, 2009, was the 'Year of the

Homecoming', the 250th anniversary of the birth of Robert Burns, when Scotland aspired to welcome 'home' as many as possible of the Scottish diaspora, the 40 million people worldwide who claimed Scottish descent. Perth & Kinross Council determined to take part fully in this project, and mounted more 'Homecoming events' than any other local authority except Edinburgh and Glasgow. Perth also wanted a 'Homecoming' for the Stone of Destiny and the Chamber of Commerce submitted a request for this to the First Minister in July 2009, on behalf of Council. But it was not successful.

The following year, Perth celebrated the 800th anniversary of its Royal Burgh charter. This had been granted by King William the Lion in 1210 and it can still be seen in Perth Museum. Big celebrations took place in Perth throughout the year, including many major events which normally rotate around different cities in the UK but which were attracted to come to Perth in that special year. The 'Homecoming of the Stone', or even an announcement that it would happen, would have greatly complemented the programme. Alas, it was not to be.

Following the success of the 800th anniversary year, Perth pursued its bid to reclaim its lost city status in the expected Queen's Diamond Jubilee celebrations of 2012. When local government was reformed in 1975, Perth was unjustly deprived of its right to call itself a city, which had flowed seamlessly from its ancient charter, granting it the status of a Royal Burgh. The campaign to restore it, like that to secure the return of the Stone of Destiny, has a long history. In 2005, Perth & Kinross Council had played a very important role in the staging of the G8 summit at The Gleneagles Hotel and had performed the functions of host for this international event superbly well. The Council believed that the restoration of city status would be an appropriate reward, and so with much pomp and ceremony, it submitted an application accordingly. Sadly, it too was ignored.

A far more ambitious city status campaign was pursued between 2010 and 2012, and in due course it was successful. That success emphasised to Perth people the importance of civic status and civic pride in promoting its economy. Although the Stone of Destiny had not featured in the campaign, the fact that Perth did become a city is thought to have been an important factor in bringing it home.

Meanwhile, the future of Perth City Hall hung in the balance. Towards the end of the twentieth century, the City Hall, which for decades had been at the centre of Perth's social life and had been staging concerts, conferences and many similar events since 1911, was at the end of its useful life. It needed a huge expenditure to bring it up to modern standards, and even with that it would have lacked the 'breakout space' and other facilities required for modern conferences and other similar events, and so it was decided to close it and build a new concert hall next to the then Perth Museum & Art Gallery (today Perth Art Gallery). In 2005, the new Perth Concert Hall was opened and the City Hall was closed.

What then to do with the City Hall – a large 'B' listed building requiring huge expenditure, whatever its ultimate purpose might be? The Council's preference was to demolish it and create a large open space between St John's Kirk and King Edward Street. This would have enhanced the setting of the mediaeval kirk and provided Perth with a central square which it has long lacked and where outdoor events could be staged. It also chimed very well with Perth's stated aim to be seen as a small European city. But it was very unpopular with the people of Perth, a huge proportion of whom seemed to have met their lifetime partners on the City Hall's dance floor. There were other problems as well. Because of the hall's listed status, the regulations demanded that it had first to be marketed to see if a viable purpose with a well-supported business plan could emerge. This was done and in 2006 a preferred bidder for a mixed retail development was selected. However, in 2009, after several extensions in the time permitted to develop the plan, the bid collapsed for lack of business and financial support.

In 2010, the Council, concerned about the public backlash against demolition, commissioned an independent assessment to determine the best future for the City Hall and its site. This confirmed that because of the huge cost of any alternative proposal, the most beneficial option was the demolition of the City Hall, and the creation of a Civic Square, and in 2011 this plan was approved at a meeting of the full Council. However, because of its listed status, permission to demolish was required from Historic Scotland, and in 2012 this was refused. Historic Scotland insisted that it should be marketed again and so, over the next four years this was done aggressively, and in total six bids were received. Independent assessors found that all but one of them, 'lacked detail in relation to proposed commercial terms, business case and funding arrangements'. Eventually, Perth Market Place Ltd was appointed to be the preferred bidder, but by 2016 the Council was informed that it had failed to meet the pre-conditions, and the appointment was withdrawn. Meanwhile, although the building was costing a great deal to maintain, it was still deteriorating steadily and its future looked very precarious.

Then, in 2016, a new factor emerged – the Tay Cities Deal. This deal, similar to arrangements in other areas of the country, promised to unlock £400 million (later increased to over £700 million) from the Scottish and UK governments for crucial infrastructure projects in Perthshire, Dundee, Angus and North East Fife. The way was open for developments far beyond what the local councils could afford.

Now, with the availability of significant financial support, Perth & Kinross Council decided to develop the City Hall as a prestigious new Museum of Mediaeval Perth with, it hoped, the Stone of Destiny as its central attraction. An architectural competition for the building was promoted and five applications were shortlisted. These were displayed for public comment, and in August of 2017, the Council accepted the design submitted by Mecanoo, a large international practice based in Manchester. Mecanoo has constructed many prestigious buildings across the world, and according to its literature, is focused on 'Architecture, Urban Planning, Landscape and Interior'. The estimated cost was £26.5 million. It was not until March 2019 that the various planning and listed building consents were issued, and still nearly two years more until, on the 23rd of December 2020, the then First Minister, Nicola Sturgeon, who was, *ex officio*, since devolution, one of the four Commissioners of the Scottish Regalia, announced at last that the Stone of Destiny would indeed be coming to Perth. She said:

> Following due consideration, the commissioners were satisfied that the proposals for Perth City Hall gave full and proper regard to the need to ensure the security and conservation of the Stone, its accessibility to the general public, and that it would be displayed in a manner in keeping with such an important cultural artefact.

Work had already started on site and has progressed steadily with an expected opening date of April 2024. At the time of writing, the development is on target and on budget. Meanwhile, designers are working on the display for the Stone of Destiny which will explain its long and sometimes controversial history. Links are also being developed between Perth Museum and the adjacent St John's Kirk, which was very much at the centre of Perth's early history, with important connections to John Knox and the Scottish Reformation and to the Stewart monarchs at the time when Perth was the capital of Scotland. After visiting the museum, tourists will be invited to walk across the square to the kirk and see the actual site where so many important events took place.

———————————————

Chapter 12
The Stone of Destiny in Literature

THE LORE surrounding the Stone of Destiny is not confined to the ancient chronicles for it still lives and breathes today. Much fiction and non-fiction has been written about the Stone of Destiny, some of it by Scotland's most prominent writers, and indeed some by European authors as well.

The Scottish academic historian and writer of historical fiction, Marie MacPherson, noted that documented doubts about the authenticity of the Stone of Destiny in Westminster go back for nearly 250 years. The earliest suggestion that the Westminster stone is a fake appeared in *The Gentleman's Magazine* in 1781. In that publication, an unidentified contributor, signing themself 'Antiquarius', explained the discrepancy between the ancient descriptions of the Stone of Destiny, and the actuality of the stone in Westminster, by postulating that the stone which Edward I took as a trophy of war was returned to Scotland in 1329 after the Treaty of Edinburgh-Northampton, and subsequently lost, and that a substitute block of sandstone was brought back to London and installed in the Coronation Chair – an unlikely explanation indeed.

A plot to remove the Stone of Destiny from Westminster on St Andrew's Day in 1932 features in *The North Wind of Love*, the fourth of Compton McKenzie's series of six novels involving the life of his semi-autobiographical character, John Ogilvie, during the first half of the twentieth century.

The Westminster raid in 1950 stimulated more interest and several novels, children's books, even science fiction, as well as many articles in magazines. The most famous author to incorporate the Stone of Destiny in his novels is Nigel Tranter. As described elsewhere in this book, the Stone of Destiny features prominently in the first and third volumes of his trilogy about Robert the Bruce – *Steps to the Empty Throne* and *The Price of the King's Peace*; and in *Kenneth*, his book about King Kenneth MacAlpin.

* * *

The Stone by Nigel Tranter

Nigel Tranter also wrote a modern novel, *The Stone*, published 1958, which had a significant effect on the mythology surrounding the Stone of Destiny. It is a rattling good tale, told in the style of John Buchan's novel, *John McNab*, and involves Sir Patrick Kincaid of Kincaid, the 17th Baronet of that Ilk, whose forbears had forfeited the Kincaid estate after backing the Stuarts in the 1745 uprising. Also involved are Roddy Roy MacGregor, a burly ex-riveter from the Glasgow shipyards, and some of his friends who were not averse to a little minor law-breaking, and a group of English students from the Oxford University Historical Society. A romantic element is provided by Jean Graham, whose father owned the Kincaid Mains farm and tenanted the surrounding land which comprised the entire Kincaid estate of Sir Patrick's ancestors.

The Oxford University Historical Society had discovered a long lost document stating that the ancient Stone of Destiny, which had been hidden from Edward I's soldiers, is buried under the floor of a doocot on the Kincaid estate. This chimed with Patrick Kincaid's family tradition, which claimed that the Stone of Destiny had been floated across the Tay from Scone, only a few miles away, and then hidden on the estate by one of his ancestors. The novel begins when Patrick reads a report in *The Scotsman* that the Oxford Society was about to mount an expedition to find the Stone of Destiny, and he decides to do what he can to thwart their plans.

He enlists Roddy MacGregor and his friends. Jean Graham also joins the team. He was fortunate that while the students were on the estate excavating the floor of a seventeenth-century doocot, without appreciating that it was too modern a construction to have been the Stone of Destiny's hiding place, Jean Graham points out a mound that was the site of a more ancient circular doocot, which had been completely demolished, with no trace remaining above ground.

The rest of the book deals with the cat and mouse matter of avoiding the students while McGregor's team dig a trench across the site of the ancient doocot, find, and with great difficulty, extract the Stone of Destiny from a deep hole where it has been hidden for nearly 700 years. Then there are accounts of several escapades, a major car crash and some lucky escapes. By this time, their activities have been reported to the authorities and the local police, as well as the Home Office in London, and Scotland Yard, are all hunting for them – although the local police are none too diligent, and occasionally looked the other way.

Eventually, with the help of a family of travelling folk, they managed to get the Stone of Destiny into the back of a horse drawn cart and take it to the Sma' Glen. There they had hoped to dump it amongst other boulders, where it would not be recognised. But fate takes a hand, and as they try to manoeuvre it into position, a clumsy move causes the stone to fall down a steep bank and land in a shallow bog at the edge of the River Almond. They watched, horrified, as mud closes over the top of the Stone of Destiny leaving nothing to see. Now only an accurate map reference can reveal where the Stone of Destiny lies, but the Oxford students, the men from the Home Office and Scotland Yard, and the local police all go away empty-handed.

And of course, Sir Patrick got the girl, and would soon become, Sir Patrick Kincaid of Kincaid, the laird of the Kincaid estate of his ancestors.

The Search for the Stone of Destiny by Pat Gerber

Although written more than 30 years ago, this is still the best book about the Stone of Destiny. Published in 1992 by journalist and novelist Pat Gerber, who had a lifetime's interest in Scottish history and in the Stone of Destiny in particular. Furthermore, it is very well illustrated by Andrew Morris.

The book is a broadbrush journalistic examination of Scottish history in relation to the Stone of Destiny – Jacob's Pillow, Alexander III, John Balliol, William Wallace, and of course Robert the Bruce. It is written from the point of view that the Stone of Destiny had been substituted by the monks of Scone Abbey. Gerber takes her readers on interesting excursions to Iona (with a chapter on Columba), Ireland, Finlaggan in Islay, and to Skye and the possible hiding place of the Stone of Destiny behind a waterfall. She visits Dunstaffnage and speculates on the possibility of inaugurations taking place there.

In a later chapter, she examines the Dunsinane story, and a letter published by The Times on New Year's Day, 1819. She notes how its widespread republication by other newspapers indicated the depth of interest in the Stone of Destiny's story at that time, right across the UK.

While modern historians tend to view the letter as a hoax, Gerber is not so sure. Excavations, even though primitive, have shown that substantial elements of the account in *The Times* letter were factual, and could hardly have been known to a prankster. (See Chapter 14.)

The Cludgie Stane of Destiny by Robbie the Pict

Robbie the Pict is an inveterate campaigner, and writer of letters to the authorities. His book, *The Cludgie Stane of Destiny*, published in 1997, consists of transcripts of some 30 letters to the police, politicians, civil servants and others, including HM the late Queen and the Dean of Westminster Abbey, spanning the years from 1993 until the Stone of Destiny's return in 1996. The underlying theme in the letters is the fact that the Stone of Destiny is indisputably stolen property, and that in Scotland there is no Statute of Limitation. This means that no matter how long it is since a theft took place, the stolen objects can never become the property of the thief (or the thief's heirs), and those handling the stolen goods can be prosecuted for reset (the dishonest possession of goods). His letters are polite and reasonable. There is no hint of aggression, nor any threats. More interesting are the replies he received, and his comments about them.

The first letter is addressed to the Chief Constable of Perthshire. It reports the theft of the Coronation Stone from the Abbey of Scone, noting that it 'is believed to have been stolen in 1296 by Edward Longshanks'. Following a very brief dismissal of his request from the Chief Superintendent of Tayside Police, he wrote to John Major, the Prime Minister, quoting a recently-published Justice Charter for Scotland which stated that, 'The People of Scotland can expect their police to detect offenders and report them to the Procurator Fiscal', and 'to act without fear, favour or prejudice'. After a delay of six weeks, he received a reply from the Scottish Office, stating that the police did not think an offence had been committed.

While Robbie's letters are generally concise, they are, nevertheless, detailed and well-researched. Of the replies, a few come into the category of peremptory dismissals, like that from the Chief of Tayside Police, but most are polite and thoughtful, and some are quite detailed. A few of the replies, like the response from Michael Forsyth, the Secretary of State for

Scotland, were written by the recipient of Robbie's missive, rather than delegated to an official.

What Robbie does not explain is the title of his book which seems unrelated to its content. *What relevance has the word 'Cludgie' to the Stone of Destiny?* The word is not derived from Gaelic and is not listed in the *Chambers Scots Dictionary*. However, it is listed as 'slang', in the *Concise Scots Dictionary*, where it is said to mean a 'water closet'. It only featured quite recently in the *Oxford English Dictionary*, where it is said to be Scots slang. In the author's experience it is most usually used to refer to a shared toilet in a tenement, especially in Glasgow. Another related meaning for the word is a 'cesspit', although this is not recorded in the *Oxford English Dictionary*, and this may be the clue to its use in the title. Those seeking to undermine the idea that the Westminster stone is the original Stone of Destiny, claim that the rings and staples that are obviously intended to enable it to be lifted, indicate that the first use of the Stone of Destiny was a cap stone for a cesspit. While it may indeed have been a cap stone above a burial vault or crypt, its great weight makes it very unlikely that it would have been a cap for a cesspit.

Monuments Celtiques by Jacques Cambray

Interest in the Stone of Destiny was not confined to Scotland. Frenchman, Jacques Cambray, in his book, *Monuments Celtiques, ou Recherche sur le Culte des Pierres*, written in 1805, claimed that he had seen the Stone of Destiny and that 'it still bore the inscription upon it, *Nic fallat fatum, Scoti quocumque locatun invenient lapidiem, regnasse tenetur ibidem*', which is precisely what John of Fordun described in his chronicle. Cambray's claim sparked considerable interest at the time and some believed that he had seen the original Stone of Destiny.

However, Cambray was writing at a time when there was a passion across Europe for all matters Druidical and Celtic. In Scotland, that was manifest by the enthusiastic reception given to the poems of Ossian, said to have been collected from Gaelic bards in the West of Scotland and the Islands, but which have since been shown to have been mostly written by their publisher, James Macpherson. Jacques Cambray was fascinated by the megaliths of Brittany and the henge monuments in England, but there is no evidence that at any time did he examine Scotland's Stone of

Destiny. In fact, his claim that he had found and deciphered an inscription on the stone in Westminster Abbey – is clearly a figment of his imagination.

The Stone of Destiny; Symbol of Nationhood
by David Breeze and Graeme Munro

This book, written by David Breeze (Chief Inspector of Ancient Monuments) and Graeme Munro (Chief Executive of Historic Scotland) is a tourist-focused book that was published by Historic Scotland in 1996 to celebrate the return of the Stone of Destiny to Scotland.[1] The authors support Aitchison's view (see below) that the stone stolen by Edward I was a Pictish royal stone which was adopted by Kenneth MacAlpin and The Scots following their victory over the Picts in 843. Nevertheless, they seem less than confident in this belief when they state that there will 'probably always be speculation as to whether Edward I took the 'real' stone in 1296'. Additionally, they provide no evidence to back up their view, save for the fair, but not conclusive, argument that if the real stone had been hidden by the monks of Scone Abbey, Abbott Henry would have produced it for the inauguration of Robert the Bruce. It is true to say, of course, that most historians believe that the Stone of Destiny was not used at Bruce's inauguration, but the record of the occasion leaves room for some doubt.

Breeze and Munro do not defend their peremptory dismissal of the evidence of the ancient chronicles and folk memory, despite many examples in history which point, although sometimes in a distorted fashion, to a kernel of truth which historians have discounted. Furthermore, they make no attempt to explain why, uniquely for an ancient Pictish stone, this one is rough and undecorated, and nor do they suggest a purpose for the staples and rings or propose a reason why a people with such well-developed metalworking skills would deface a revered icon with such clumsy ironwork.

Academic Publications

For an item of such huge cultural significance both for Scotland and England and indeed Ireland, there has been a strange dearth of modern academic investigation into both the source and history of the Stone of Destiny.

---

1 David Breeze co-edited, and Graeme Munro contributed to the book, *The Stone of Destiny: Artefact and Icon*, which is also reviewed in this chapter.

Where are the books, the articles in academic journals, and the PhD theses about the Stone of Destiny and The Scots? In the last 150 years, there have been only two significant academic publications on this topic. This would appear to be inexplicable given Scotland's many departments of history and Edinburgh's foremost School of Scottish Studies.

Concern about this matter is not recent. William F Skene in his paper to the Society of Antiquaries of Scotland in 1869, referred to earlier, noted that the legend of the Stone was:

> a solitary waif from the sea of myth and fable, [with] which modern criticism has hardly ventured to meddle, and which modern scepticism has not cared to question.

He then went on to review, comprehensively, its history and that of The Scots, as recorded in the various legends and chronicles. Nevertheless, with regard to The Scots he concluded:

> their wanderings, like those of the tribes with whom they are associated, are nothing but myth and fable.

And so far as the Stone of Destiny was concerned, he believed that prior to its theft by Edward I, it:

> never was anywhere but at Scone.[2]

Skene was, however, writing over 150 years ago, and the enormous progress of Celtic studies in recent years has seen a reappraisal of many of his conclusions, although the jury is still out in relation to the Stone of Destiny itself.

There are two notable exceptions to the lack of modern scholarly study of the Stone of Destiny: Nick Aitchison, *Scotland's Stone of Destiny: Myth, History and Nationhood* (The History Press, 2000) and Richard Welander, David J Breeze and Thomas Owen Clancy (eds), *The Stone of Destiny: Artefact and Icon* (Society of Antiquaries of Scotland, 2003).

---

2 Skene, *The Coronation Stone.*

Scotland's Stone of Destiny: Myth, History and Nationhood by Nick Aitchison

This encyclopaedic volume by Nick Aitchison is the first modern, fully-researched and illustrated study of the history and mythology of the Stone of Destiny and its cultural significance. Aitchison describes the Stone of Destiny in careful detail and speculates on possible earlier functions that it may have had and devotes a long chapter to a discussion about its authenticity. In a later chapter, he traces the development of Scone as a Pictish royal centre before its takeover by The Scots and bemoans the lack of significant archaeological excavations at the site of the Abbey of Scone. Finally, he describes in some detail the return of the Stone of Destiny to Edinburgh from Westminster Abbey.

Aitchison believes the Stone of Destiny is an example of an origin myth. It is said that origin myths enabled ancient peoples, such as The Scots, to explain where they had come from and how they had got their name. Aitchison discounts all the evidence that the stone used to inaugurate Kenneth MacAlpin's heirs up to John Balliol in 1292 was different from the Stone of Scone. Aitchison's central conclusion, like that of W F Skene, is that the stone removed by Edward I was a royal inaugural stone upon which the Picts had crowned their kings for generations prior to 843. Following the defeat of the Picts by Kenneth MacAlpin, Aitchison believes that the Stone of Destiny was adopted by The Scots and used to inaugurate MacAlpin's successors in order to appease the national sentiments of the defeated Picts and perhaps hasten their integration into a single Scots nation. Aitcheson's assertion that the stone removed to Westminster Abbey was an ancient Pictish inaugural stone is backed by most academics, historians and archaeologists.

The Stone of Destiny: Artefact and Icon edited by Richard Welander, David J Breeze and Thomas Owen Clancy

The fortnight between the return of the Stone of Destiny to Scotland on the 15th of November and its official handover to the Commissioners of the Regalia in Edinburgh Castle on St Andrew's Day, the 30th of that month, presented the authorities with the first ever opportunity to examine it in minute detail. This was important for historical and archaeological reasons, and also because there was persistent speculation about possible substitution in 1951 by the Glasgow students, or in 1296 by the monks of Scone Abbey, or indeed by Kenneth MacAlpin. Interest in the Stone of Destiny had grown considerably since John Major's promise to return it to Scotland in 1996, and it was obviously desirable to make the most of the opportunity to have Scottish experts examine the Stone of Destiny in Scotland. The results of these investigations were presented at a conference organised by the Society of Antiquaries of Scotland on the 10th of May 1997. Its purpose was to celebrate the return of the Stone of Destiny to Scotland.

The book, *The Stone of Destiny: Artefact and Icon*, a very substantial and important publication, grew out of that conference. It is far more than a report of the conference proceedings because the opportunity was taken to expand the remit of the conference to include discussions about the rituals, thrones and other matters relating to inaugurations both in Scotland and Ireland and also elsewhere. And so the book has an introduction, six sections comprising seventeen profusely-illustrated chapters written by twenty contributors and a foreword by Lord Cullen. This accounts for the delay in its publication which was not until 2003, seven years after the return of the Stone of Destiny and six years after the conference on which it was based.

Several of the contributions to the book relate to cultural and procedural matters and are not particularly relevant to the Stone of Destiny. Among these are the six chapters of Section 2 which cover inauguration rituals, including the use of sacred stones and chairs, elsewhere in Scotland, in Ireland and on the Continent. Likewise, a chapter in Section 3 (Scone) – *'Before Coronation: Making a King at Scone in the Thirteenth Century'* and another in in Section 4 ('The Taking of the Stone') – *'A 'Sign of Victory'; the Coronation Chair, its manufacture, setting and symbolism'* – do not deal with the Stone of Destiny itself. The remaining chapters which are particularly useful when trying to elucidate the origin and history of the Stone of Destiny are discussed below.

Introduction

David Breeze describes the Stone of Destiny's geology, and its 'archaeology' – by which he means the insertion of the iron staples and rings and the tooling on its surface. To account for the smoothness of the top surface, he suggests that it may have been 'placed on the floor of the church and knelt on or kissed by pilgrims'.

While Breeze restates his view, previously expressed in the book, *Scotland's Stone of Destiny*, that the stone now in Perth was not exchanged prior to its acquisition by Edward I's soldiers, he does not entirely dismiss the possibility that a substitution may have been engineered by Abbott Henry and the monks of Scone Abbey. Nevertheless, he gives five reasons why he believes this did not happen. These are:

1. He notes that a number of senior clerics and courtiers who had attended the inauguration of John Balliol might have been expected to be able to verify the authenticity of the Stone.

2. If Abbott Hendry had hidden the Stone, he would have produced it for Bruce's inauguration.

3. Breeze does not believe that because Abbott Henry did have time to hide the Stone, he would have done so. He notes that those guarding the Honours of Scotland had similar warnings of Edward's approach, but they did not attempt to conceal them.

4. He notes that the Stone is a complex object (although he does not explain what that means) and could not have been created by Abbott Henry at short notice.

5. The Stone is too complex an object to have been in use elsewhere in Scone in 1296.

6. The Stone is too unprepossessing an object to have been acceptable to Edward I unless it was known to be the genuine Stone.

Only the first two of these reasons are persuasive, but they are not conclusive. Breeze acknowledges that the Stone would have been covered, indeed obscured, by rich cloths, but he does not mention that, as noted in

Chapter 4, the ceremony was not held outside, as was usual, but inside the Abbey church. This was small and would have been ill lit and, it being the end of November, the light inside the building would have been poor. Under these circumstances those attending the inauguration of Balliol may hardly have noticed the Stone of Destiny, which was not in any way controversial at the time, and when they saw it again in London some time later, they may not have realised that it was different from the one they had encountered in Scone. Even if some of them did have doubts, they may have considered it wise to keep quiet.

If indeed the Stone had been exchanged by Abbott Henry, the reason why it was not produced for the inauguration of Robert the Bruce, may have been because it had been hidden at some distance from Scone, as recounted in Chapter 13, and with Bruce in a hurry, there was not time to get it. Furthermore, from a distance in time of more than 700 years it is impossible to know what other obstacles there may have been to producing the Stone for Bruce's inauguration.

The fact that those guarding the Honours of Scotland in Edinburgh did not attempt to hide them may have been because Edinburgh would have been thronged with English soldiers and other partisans, which would have made the acts of concealing and substituting such obvious items as the the Crown, Sceptre and the Sword of State impossible. This was not the situation in remote Scone.

The fact that the Stone is a complex object is not relevant with regard to its concealment or otherwise by Abbott Henry, nor is speculation about its use elsewhere at that time.

Finally, Breeze believed correctly that Edward was no fool and that 'it would have been a very brave man who attempted to fob off this intelligent yet volatile Plantagenet with such an unprepossessing object, unless it was genuine'. The probability is that Abbott Henry was indeed a very brave man, whose Abbey suffered grievously for his bravery.

Neither Breeze nor any of his co-editors address the possibility that the Stone might have been exchanged. They do not refer to the work by James Richardson, a former Inspector of Ancient Monuments in Scotland, on the Great Seals of the King of Scotland, noted in Chapter 4, which suggests that the stone used at Balliol's inauguration was larger and a different shape from the one stolen. Nor do they mention the only contemporary description of the Stone by Canon Walter of Guisborough which confirms Richardson's hypothesis. Lastly, they do not discuss nor even mention the doubts expressed in the volume they edited by contributors Peter Hill and Dauvit Broun.

Section 1: The Stone as an Object
Chapter 1: The Stone of Destiny Examined –
An Overview and Discussion.

The first detailed examination of the Stone of Destiny, carried out by a specialist stonemason, was made by Peter Hill, a stone and historic buildings consultant from London. Hill presented his findings at the one-day conference and they are recorded in the first chapter of Section 1 of the account of the conference.

Diagrammatic sketch of the side view of the shortened Stone of Destiny showing the present and original outlines of the Stone and the iron staple surrounded by lead with a dotted line showing where it had been fitted.

Hill's description of the Stone of Destiny is meticulous and technical. He was able to determine the various stonemason's tools used, and detect the fact that the work on the upper surface of the Stone was apparently started by a skilled stonemason, and then abandoned, but taken up later by a less-skilled craftsman. He suggests that the most likely use of the Stone of Destiny at the stage in its history, before it was pressed into service as a royal inaugural stone, was as part of a long step, with other stones at each end. The smoothness of the upper surface indicates that this function must have lasted for a long time, and that the Stone of Destiny was probably outside.

Hill postulates that at some time after the staples and rings were inserted the Stone of Destiny was cut down in length, losing around two or three centimetres at each end. He does not offer any reason why or when this happened.

The provision of the staples and rings suggests that it was anticipated that the Stone of Destiny would be moved reasonably frequently, and that its ends were not accessible to permit it to be lifted by grasping with the hands. He also notes that the space that the Stone of Destiny might have occupied in the floor of the church is too narrow to permit easy access to a storage cellar or burial vault. However, an opening in the floor measuring a little more than 670 mm by 420 mm could permit occasional access by a reasonably athletic individual, to a crypt below.

Hill's paper concludes with a detailed evaluation of Pictish stones, in particular those at nearby Meigle and at Abernethy and St Vigeans. He states that although some have suggested that the Stone of Destiny has a Pictish origin: 'It bears no resemblance whatsoever to known Pictish stonework'. He continues to note that the craftsmanship exhibited on the Stone of Destiny is at best 'workmanlike', compared to: 'the almost staggering care and skill shown on the Pictish stones'.

The implication is that the stone uplifted for Edward I was not a stone that had been used at earlier Pictish ceremonies and inaugurations and, therefore, had not been expropriated by Kenneth MacAlpin. The unstated conclusion is that the stone used to inaugurate generations of Kings of Scots from MacAlpin's time to John Balliol in 1292 was not the stone taken in 1296, and therefore that Edward must have been deceived. It is pertinent to wonder why this obvious conclusion is not included in the contribution.

Chapter 2: The Geology of the Stone of Destiny

In this contribution, Emrys Phillips of the British Geological Survey and his colleagues begin by reviewing previous geological examinations of the Stone.

Writing in 1819 and 1824, John MacCulloch, one of the pioneers of Scottish geology, described the Stone of Destiny and noted its similarity to the stone which forms the doorway of Dunstaffnage Castle, although it was, he stated, 'impossible to fix precisely the original source'. In 1937, a microscopic examination of chips and grains obtained when the Stone of Destiny was cleaned in 1865 did not advance matters. However, by 1998, geological opinion, based on re-examining the earlier evidence, favoured the Scone/Perth area and it was considered that a further investigation might be helpful.

And so in 1998, two years after the Stone of Destiny had been installed in Edinburgh Castle, Historic Scotland authorised a further technical examination to record its geological features. Among the objectives was to determine if the location of the outcrop of sandstone from which the Stone of Destiny was originally quarried could be identified, as this would have important implications regarding its history. And so Phillips was commissioned to carry out another analysis using the most up-to-date scientific methods.

Taking a chip of stone which had been collected in 1865, and examining it microscopically using the most modern techniques, the petrologists were able to compare the composition of the Westminster stone with rock formations in Scone, in the Oban/Lorne area of Argyll, and in other parts of the stratum of Old Red Sandstone which lies across Scotland between the Firths of Tay and Clyde. They concluded that 'the lithology of the Stone is indeed comparable with the Lower Old Red Sandstone of the Perth area...and with samples from the old quarries at Quarrymill'. Furthermore, they dismissed the possibility that the stone came from any of the other areas that they examined.

These studies confirmed that the Stone had not been substituted by a copy stone in 1951, and was indeed the one that had lain undisturbed in Westminster Abbey for the seven centuries since Edward I had installed it. Just as certain, however, the results showed that the Stone of Destiny could not have originated in Ireland, Spain or the Middle East, although, interestingly, this conclusion is not mentioned. Skene had been right when he stated in 1869 that the Stone of Destiny, 'had never been anywhere but Scone'.

Section 2: Inaugurations and Symbols of Dominion
Section 3: Scone
Chapter 1: Before Coronation:
Making a King at Scone in the Thirteenth Century

This chapter by A A M Duncan deals with developments in the inauguration ceremonies during the thirteenth century, prior to the inauguration of John Balliol in 1292.

Chapter 2: The Buildings Old Scone

Richard Fawcett describes the building and fortunes of Scone Abbey from its founding in around 1115 to its destruction during the Reformation in 1559. In this chapter, Fawcett notes that there may not have been much damage when the Stone of Destiny was removed from Scone Abbey in 1296, but that on the return of Edward's soldiers in 1298, the roofs and ceilings of the major buildings of the Abbey complex were badly vandalised. He does not speculate on the reason for the return visit by Edward's soldiers and in particular does not relate it to the possibility that the stone had been switched.

In due course, the damage was repaired and Scone Abbey became an important destination for pilgrimages during the last century of its existence.

Section 4: The Taking of the Stone

Chapter 1: The Origin of the Stone of Scone as a National Icon

In this chapter, Dauvit Broun concentrates on the changing rituals which had developed in Scone, in particular relating to the inauguration of Alexander III in 1249. However, in a later part of the chapter, more relevant to the subject of this book, he reviews the legend of the Stone of Destiny going back to Simon Brecc. He refers mainly to John of Fordun's chronicle, but notes that Fordun's source was a lost chronicle dating from around 1214, which itself was probably based on a lost saint's life dating from the twelfth century or even earlier. Broun emphasises the Stone of Destiny's historical Irish, rather than Pictish origin, and he is the only contributor to the book to do so.

> Although the Stone of Scone symbolised the kingship's antiquity it was evidently still regarded in the thirteenth century as a tangible token of the kingdom's Irish identity.

A stone with an Irish identity could not have been quarried at Scone. In Broun's view, Alba was an ancient territory which, prior to 843, had comprised two kingdoms of roughly equal age – the large Pictish kingdom in the east and the much smaller Scots kingdom in the west founded by Fergus Mòr mac Eric in 500. Broun concludes:

It may be guessed that the Pictish kingdom lived on in Scone's status as the royal centre of Alba, and that the kingship established by Fergus was represented by the Stone itself.

As with Hill's contribution, the implication is that the stone that Edward I had brought to London is not the original Stone of Destiny from Ireland, and that the monks of Scone Abbey must have substituted the ancient stone with a block of local sandstone from Quarrymill. It is surprising that this is not stated explicitly, nor even discussed.

Chapter 2: The Removal of the Stone and
Attempts at Recovery, to 1328

In this contribution, G W S Barrow recounts the early political attempts by The Scots to recover the Stone of Destiny following the death of Edward I. He remarks that in 1324 The Scots did try strenuously to have the Stone of Destiny returned, and that they might indeed have been successful were it not for their associated demand for unconditional recognition of the nation's independence. Edward II was forever an inadequate shadow of his martial father, especially since Bannockburn. Because granting Scotland's independence would emphasise that impression, unconditional recognition was just not acceptable. However, by the time of the Treaty of Edinburgh-Northampton in 1328, Edward II had been deposed and subsequently murdered, and Edward III was on the throne, and the English Parliament agreed to recognise Scotland's independence. The Stone of Destiny is not mentioned in this treaty, but neither were other deeply venerated items, notably the Black Rood of St Margaret, and these were returned to Scotland. Barrow believes that the Stone of Destiny would also have been included, but that its return was blocked by the London mob, encouraged no doubt, by the Abbot of Westminster Abbey.

Section 5: The Return
Chapter 1: The Stone of Destiny in Modern Times

Graeme Munro, at that time Director and Chief Executive of Historic Scotland, reviews the Parliamentary debates on the Stone of Destiny from 1924 until 1950, and then retells the story of the raid on the Abbey by the Glasgow students. He also reviews the Cabinet discussions which followed the raid. These were considered to be so sensitive that they were not released until 1996.

Chapter 2: The Events of 1996

Richard Wellender, one of the editors of the book, recounts the events following the announcement that the Stone of Destiny was to return to Scotland, and describes in detail the journey from the throne in Westminster Abbey to the Crown Room in Edinburgh Castle.

Section 6: Envoi

This final brief section is in fact a fairly critical review of the book by Nick Aitchison.⁻

Discussion

Philips and his team confirmed that the Stone of Destiny was indisputably of local origin. Hill doubted the claim that the stone that Edward I had seized was Pictish, and Broun concluded that there was indeed an 'Irish' Stone which represented the continuing traditions of The Scots of Dàl Riada, and was still at Scone in the thirteenth century, and presumably used at John Balliol's inauguration. His unstated implication is that this 'Irish' stone must, therefore, have been exchanged by the monks of Scone Abbey to deceive Edward's men.

The absence of a discussion or an overall conclusion at the end of the book may be because there were irreconcilable differences of opinion among the contributors and the editors.

Chapter 13
The Composition and Origin of the Stone of Scone

FOLLOWING THE RAID on Scone Abbey, the Stone of Destiny was taken to Edinburgh where it remained for some time, before eventually getting to London in 1297. There, it was incorporated into the wooden throne, which had been constructed specifically for it, and placed in St Edward the Confessor's chapel behind the High Altar of Westminster Abbey.

No doubt it was 'dusted down' prior to coronations, but for many centuries there appears to have been little interest in the Stone of Destiny itself, its composition or its origin. In this sceptical era it is difficult to appreciate that the general consensus until modern times was that the Stone of Destiny was Middle Eastern in origin. There were isolated reports of examinations of it dating back to 1682, and some doubts about its origin were expressed. In 1760, Richard Pococke, the Bishop of Ossory (in Ireland), offered the first suggestion that the Stone of Destiny originated in Scotland rather than the Middle East. Pococke believed that the Stone of Destiny consisted of Scottish granite. It was not until 1819 that the composition of the Stone of Destiny was correctly identified as sandstone. Remarkably, the first time the Stone of Destiny was actually removed from its housing in the throne for a proper examination was not until 1865 when it was examined by the Scottish Geologist, Sir Andrew Ramsay, the director of the Geological Survey of Great Britain. Ramsay confirmed that it was a reddish sandstone with embedded pebbles, some of which were quartz, and there were also some flakes of mica. He noted that it was 'possibly prepared as a building block'. Chips and grains of sandstone brushed from the surface of the Stone of Destiny at that time were retained and some of them were used by Emrys Philips many years later, in 1998, to confirm its composition and source. At that time, it was noted that outcrops of a similar type of rock occurred in the Oban area, in particular around Dunstaffnage Castle, which itself is partly built of that particular stone and so a Scottish origin of the Stone of Destiny was suggested once again.

Nevertheless, it was still assumed by most of the antiquarians, and even geologists, that it had come from the Middle East. Indeed, as recently as 1902, the Reverend John H Allen stated that there was 'no rock like it in England, Ireland or Scotland' but that there was 'a stratum of sandstone near the Dead Sea just like this stone'.[1] In fact, however, we know now that there is a broad seam of Devonian Old Red Sandstone running from the North Sea coast of Scotland, north of the mouth of the River Tay, through Perth and Scone to the Clyde estuary, and some other more isolated outcrops, one of which is in the Oban area of Argyll. Only in the Perth area, however, are the deposits substantial enough to allow for the quarrying of blocks of stone as large as the Stone of Destiny.

In 1937, King George VI's coronation generated renewed interest in the Stone of Destiny. By that time, informed opinion had hardened in favour of Old Red Sandstone, but erroneously believed that it came from the Argyll outcrop near Oban, and in particular from the area around Dunstaffnage Castle. This chimed well with that element of the legend that claimed that the Stone of Destiny had been kept at Dunstaffnage but ignored the main thrust of the same tradition which was that it had been brought there from Ireland, via Iona, and not that it had originated from the rocks around the castle. Some geologists noted that the Stone of Destiny could well have come from the area around Scone, but at that time there was no way of proving it precisely.

As detailed in Chapter 12, the issue has now been resolved conclusively by Emrys Philips and his colleagues. There is no doubt that the Stone was sourced from a quarry alongside the Annaty Burn at Kincarrathie about a mile from Scone Abbey, and that it was not substituted while it was in Scotland following the raid by the Glasgow students. The fact that this stone has a local source means, of course, that it could not have been the stone that featured in the Scottish and Irish chronicles. These allege that it had come to Argyll from Ireland, probably from Spain, and perhaps even from the Middle East, and then brought to Scone by Kenneth MacAlpin in 850. At some time, therefore, between 843 and 1296, the original Irish Stone of Destiny was exchanged for a local block of sandstone from Scone. *The question is, when and under what circumstances did that happen?*

---

1 Allen was an American minister associated with the concept of British Israelism. His influential book, *Judah's Sceptre and Joseph's Birthright*, which went to many reprints, promoted the hypothesis that the Anglo-Saxon-Celtic peoples of the British Empire were descended from the House of Israel, and as such were among God's chosen people.

In modern Scotland there are two schools of thought about these matters. There are those who believe that the real Stone of Destiny which had been brought from Ireland, was exchanged for a block of local sandstone by the monks of Scone Abbey to deceive Edward I. It appears that the stone, now more appropriately referred to as the Stone of Scone, was hastily conscripted by Abbott Henry for 'national service', notwithstanding its inappropriate appearance. The only reasonable argument against this view is that if the monks had hidden the real stone, it would have been brought out of hiding for the inauguration of Robert the Bruce. Historians generally believe that that did not happen, but the record of the occasion is ambiguous.

Most academics, on the other hand (notably Nick Aitchison), believe that the Stone of Scone was originally a Pictish stone, which had been used by the Picts at royal inaugurations and on judicial occasions before their defeat by Kenneth MacAlpin, and then 'adopted' by MacAlpin to appease the Picts and ease their assimilation into the dominant Gaelic culture.

There are, however, significant arguments against this view of history. There is no tradition, nor any corroborating evidence for it. Furthermore, the conquest of the Picts by The Scots was a total, and probably brutal, military and eventual cultural takeover, resulting in the supremacy of Gaelic and the extinction of the Pictish language and the loss of its script. It seems unlikely that such a mismatched exchange of royal icons would be contemplated by the conquering Scots, or appreciated by the defeated Picts.

If the Stone of Scone had indeed been exchanged by the monks of Scone Abbey, it is certain that it was not quarried for that purpose. There would have been neither the time nor a reason to carve grooves in it or disfigure it with iron staples and rings. *So where had it been, and what was its purpose previously?* It may have been a block of construction stone, perhaps abandoned as unsuitable because it was found to have a flaw and left over or unused from a previous building project, possibly even the original Abbey itself nearly two centuries earlier in 1115. However, the tooling on the top surface, and the rings and links indicate that, in the meantime, it may have had an interesting history, and perhaps more than one use.

Hill points out that the wear on the top surface indicates that it was probably used outside as part of a long step and that it had 'experienced considerable traffic'. The possibility that it had been a step at one time was also suggested by Historic Scotland in their note to the Knights Templar, although they suggested that originally it may have been part of a circular staircase: 'The left foot wear on one side of the stone appears to reflect its use as a step in a cylindrical staircase'.

Another possibility is that it may have been a cap stone over a vault beneath the floor of the Abbey church in Scone which could be lifted up to give access to a space below. However, the access would have been very limited; just enough to allow an athletic individual to slip through, but not enough for a coffin, and so if indeed a crypt did exist beneath the church there must have been another entrance. There had been a number of important burials in Scone Abbey including that of Maud, Countess of Huntingdon and Queen of David I, who died in 1130, and these graves would certainly have been in the church.

If it was a cap stone that would explain the slightly tapered shape, and the fact that the links and rings are countersunk into the end and top surfaces of the stone to enable it to be placed neatly into the floor, preserve a level surface, and yet facilitate the lifting of the stone. It would also account for the wear on the top of the stone where it was walked upon. However, no explanation for the grooves cut in the top surface has ever been forthcoming.

Whatever the history of the Stone of Scone, it seems implausible to suggest that MacAlpin and his Scots people would discard their own ancient Stone of Destiny, and with it jettison their traditions and the folk memory of a sacred inaugural icon dating back many centuries which they had brought with them, certainly from Ireland, and perhaps from Spain or even the Middle East. In its place, there was to be a Pictish substitute of uncertain origin, devoid of symbolic carvings and adulterated with iron rings and staples. It also seems very improbable that MacAlpin or his successors would wish to adopt such a utilitarian object, nor is it credible to suggest that if he decided that he needed an inaugural stone, he would arrange for one to be quarried from Kincarrathie, and mutilated with basic iron staples, links and rings.

It is also implausible to suggest that the Picts would have as an important royal icon an object so lacking in symbolism. As Peter Hill states, the Picts had a long tradition of intricate carvings on stone and these can seen throughout Scotland, and especially in the east of the country. At Meigle Museum, some 15 miles northeast of Scone, there is a collection of Pictish carved stones, some of them very finely worked. Most of them are from the eighth and ninth centuries, just at the time of MacAlpin's conquest of Pictland.

A particular example of the finest Pictish art is the St Andrews Sarcophagus.[2] This is exhibited in the St Andrews Cathedral museum, and is one of the best-preserved examples of Pictish carving. It has been executed with exquisite craftsmanship, and has fortunately survived with very little damage. Historians believe that it was probably a burial cist for the son of the Pictish King Fergus, King Oengus, who died in 761.

The St Andrews Sarcophagus. Its intricate design provides scholars with an insight into the beliefs and aspirations of the Picts of the eighth and ninth centuries, at about the time of the brutal subjugation by MacAlpin of the Picts at Scone.

Another example was discovered recently in the bed of the burn at Forteviot, where there was a Pictish royal palace which was also used by MacAlpin, and indeed, it is where he died. It is part of an intricately carved stone arch, probably from a royal chapel within the palace, and it is now displayed in the National Museum of Scotland in Edinburgh.

---

2 In a remarkable coincidence the St Andrews Sarcophagus almost 'met' the Stone of Destiny. In November 1996, when the stone was to be transported from Westminster to Edinburgh, the vehicle which was sent to bring it north was used to take the St Andrews Sarcophagus south to the British Museum, where it was the centre piece of an exhibition, 'Heirs of Rome'. It was the first time the sarcophagus had left Scotland since its discovery in 1833, and indeed the first time since it was created more than a thousand years earlier.

*A highly-decorated stone arch from a Pictish royal chapel,
found at Forteviot, near Perth.*

These examples and other exquisitely decorated Pictish stones of the same era, demonstrate that at the time of MacAlpin's victory, the Picts were superb craftsmen in stone. And not only in stone, for the Picts were also skilled metalsmiths, capable of manufacturing everything from delicate brooches to heavy neck chains. At the important Pictish hillfort at King's Seat, Dunkeld, just 12 miles north of Scone, evidence from the discovery of crucibles and moulds which were used for smelting metal ores indicates that, by the seventh century, Picts were producing items of bronze, brass and even silver. In addition, finds at King's Seat and at other Pictish settlements in the area demonstrate that the Picts were trading as far away as France.

There is no doubt that the Picts were a skilled, cultured people and so it seems inconceivable that a stone which would be used on very important royal occasions would not only be so unadorned, but also mutilated with crude iron staples, links and rings, which have no obvious royal connection and for which no civic purpose or religious symbolism has been suggested.

Conclusion

To summarise, the inescapable conclusion is that the monks of the Abbey, having been warned that Edward's soldiers would be coming for the Stone of Destiny, looked around for a substitute stone of an appropriate size, and pressed into service the stone now revered as the Stone of Destiny, but which should be called, more correctly, the Stone of Scone.

If this is the case, it is highly probable that the real Stone of Destiny brought by Kenneth MacAlpin to Scone from Dàl Riada in the west, was hidden somewhere, probably not very far from Scone, and it has not yet been discovered. It is an exciting prospect, indeed, made more intriguing by the fact that the site of Scone Abbey has never been properly excavated.

Chapter 14
Where is the Real Stone of Destiny?

W E H A V E S E E N that the stone which rested in Westminster Abbey for 700 years did not come from Ireland or Galicia, or indeed from the Middle East but was a block of local Scone sandstone, and that this contradicts the accounts in all of the various chronicles. In recent years, the prevailing academic opinion has favoured the explanation that it was a Pictish royal stone that had been adopted by Kenneth McAlpin in order to smooth the takeover of Pictland and it was used to inaugurate his successors until Edward I stole it in 1296.

This view of history has been challenged by Dauvit Broun and by Peter Hill in their contributions to *The Stone of Destiny, Artefact & Icon*, and by a consensus of other historians, authors and antiquarians. They are inclined to accept the legends and folk memory that the real Stone of Destiny, which was brought from Ireland to Argyll, was taken to Scone by MacAlpin and used until the inauguration of MacAlpin's successors up to that of Balliol in 1292. With Edward I's soldiers approaching Scone they believe it was exchanged for the block of local sandstone by the monks of Scone Abbey. If that did happen it is right to consider where that original Stone of Destiny might be.

What Should We Be Looking For?

Legendary descriptions of the Stone of Destiny suggest that we should be looking for something quite different from the rough sandstone block that has attracted such veneration over the centuries. Almost certainly, the real Stone of Destiny was much larger, probably black and consisting of marble or basalt, and perhaps with carved decorations and inscriptions upon it. Every one of the Scottish thrones, which are illustrated on the great seals of The Scots monarchs from the eleventh to the thirteenth century, was of a size to accommodate a stone approximately 420 mm to 508 mm high, and probably 381 mm to 457 mm square in section. This is important because this feature of the illustrations of the thrones is consistent, whereas other attributes depicted on the seals vary considerably. Such a stone is not only larger and heavier than the Stone of Scone, but a completely different shape. The Kings of Scots, as depicted on their seals, do not appear to be sitting on a stone of the size and shape of the Stone of Scone, which is only 280 mm high. Furthermore, there is no evidence in the illustrations of any of the seals that the stone has been raised to a more appropriate height in the way that it has been raised on four lion feet below the throne in Westminster.

Where Might the Stone of Destiny Have Been Hidden?

Scone Palace Grounds and the Site of the Abbey

There is the distinct likelihood that the Stone of Destiny was hidden locally within the grounds of the Abbey and if so, it is almost certain that it will be there still, either buried in the vicinity of the Abbey, or perhaps incorporated into the foundations of Scone Palace. A mob inspired by John Knox destroyed the Abbey during the Reformation in 1559, and its monks and priests were dispersed. What remained of the buildings and the land, the source of its wealth, were forfeited to the Crown (James VI), and, in 1580, granted to William Ruthven of Huntingtower, who became the first Earl of Gowrie. He built the first Scone Palace in the 1580s reusing many of the stones from the ruined abbey. Compared with today, the perception of items of historical importance was very different in the sixteenth century, and so if the Stone of Destiny was in the vicinity of the Abbey, and not completely hidden, it may well have been used as an important building block, perhaps a corner stone, for the new palace.

The first Scone Palace lasted for over 300 years, until 1796. By then, it was owned by the Murray family, and David Murray, the 3rd Earl of Mansfield, engaged the architect, William Atkinson, to rebuild his Scone family home as a magnificent gothic palace. Importantly, the footprint of the new palace was roughly the same as its predecessor, so elements of the mediaeval house have survived. If the Stone of Destiny was not used for the first building, it might have been requisitioned for its successor. It is also possible, of course, that if it was buried adequately, it may have been undisturbed since 1296, and if so it will still be there. No thorough archaeological excavation of the site has ever been undertaken.

* * *

The Sleat Peninsula of Skye

There is a tradition that as he lay dying, King Robert the Bruce summoned Angus Ogg MacDonald (Aonghus Òg Mac Domhnaill), the younger son of Angus Moray MacDonald, the Chief of Clan Donald of the Isles, to his bedside.[1] Clan Donald had been in the Balliol camp in the first years of the fourteenth century, but after Bruce seized the throne in 1306 they perceived potential gains of land and influence at the expense of their local MacDougall rivals, and they become strong supporters of the Bruce cause. Angus Ogg himself had led a large contingent of men from the Isles to the Battle of Bannockburn, where they had played a vital part in the victory. In 1329, as his life was ebbing away, Bruce was said to have been concerned that if the location of the Stone of Destiny became known to the English monarchy, an army would be dispatched north to get it. Consequently, he entrusted the Stone of Destiny to the safekeeping of the MacDonalds of the Isles. He hoped that a remote location, and the strong support for his cause among the local people of the Isles, would secure its safety.

At the end of the third part of his trilogy about Robert the Bruce, *The Price of the King's Peace* (first published in 1970), Nigel Tranter used this tradition to make compelling historical fiction out of the deathbed scene at Cardross Castle on the north bank of the Clyde. Bruce, knowing that he was dying, summoned his three most trusted lieutenants, Thomas Randolph, James Douglas and Angus Ogg. To Randolph, the wisest head, he entrusted the government of his kingdom on behalf of his five-year-old son, the future King David II. To the Black Douglas, his most loyal comrade on the battlefield, his final request was to extract his heart from its mortal cage, and take it on a crusade. And to Angus Ogg, from the Islands in the west, he entrusted the safe keeping of the Stone of Destiny, with the command to take it to the Hebrides until Scotland was free of the English threat.

Bruce's concern about the threat from England was well-founded. In 1332, just three years after his death, with his eight-year-old son, David II, now on the throne and the governance of the country in the hands of feuding regents, Edward Balliol, the son of the former King John Balliol,

---

1   The author can trace his own family history back through twenty generations to Angus Ogg, but sadly he is not party to any secret about where the Stone of Destiny may be.

perceived an opportunity to invade Scotland, and claim sovereignty. He sailed his force up the North Sea to the River Tay. The invaders landed on the south bank of the river about 3 miles from Perth, at the site where Elcho Castle now stands, and marched towards the city. Balliol defeated the Scots at the Battle of Dupplin Moor, just south of Perth, after which the city fell without resistance. In due course, having acknowledged Edward II as his overlord, Edward Balliol was crowned at Scone (but not, of course, on the Stone of Destiny). Nevertheless, he did not achieve full control over Scotland, and his rule effectively ended three years later in 1335 following his defeat at the Battle of Culblean, in Aberdeenshire. His reign was not legitimised, and his name does not appear in the official list of Scottish kings.

The legend of the Stone of Destiny tells that Angus Ogg took it to the MacDonald fortress on Eilean Mòr (the Big Island) in Loch Finlaggan in the centre of the Island of Islay where the MacDonalds, the Lords of the Isles, ruled the Inner Hebrides like kings in their own right. Angus Ogg himself did not survive long after Bruce, and died at Finlaggan in 1329. He was buried on Iona. The legend, however, continues, and it is said that following the forfeiture of the Lords of the Isles by James IV in 1493, the Stone of Destiny was brought by the MacDonalds from Islay to their territory on the peninsula of Sleat on Skye, where in due course it was hidden in a cave behind a waterfall. It is claimed that it is there still.

This story of the Skye Stone was quickened in 1959 by a letter, copies of which were sent to Nigel Tranter and others. It was written on headed notepaper and signed by someone who called himself Mr C Iain Alasdair Macdonald. Despite strenuous efforts, it has proved impossible to identify or trace this individual, and many believe that the letters were a hoax. Nevertheless, they reinforced the belief that the Stone of Destiny was hidden on Skye, and that has proved to be a persistent tradition even in the absence of any corroborating evidence.

In his letters, Macdonald expounds that he was born in India and served in the British forces during the Second World War, but came back to the UK in 1946, and was living in Brighton. In his first letter he begins:

> I have in my possession an antique chest which has been handed down through generations of Macdonalds of the Isles,

and which dates back to Somerled, Regulus of the Isles...In the secret place on Skye where the chest was originally hidden is also 'The Stone', which I believe is the Stone of Destiny.

In his next letter, he claims that he is now the 'custodian of the Stone' and 'has seen it himself and knows its hiding place on Skye'. He tells how he was brought from India by his father and grandfather and taken to Skye:

> ...to the secret hiding place and shown the Stone, which I sat on and was made to take an oath to guard its secret whereabouts and also to screen my successor. So well is it hidden that I was taken four times along the secret route, and then find my own way four times to make sure that I had a clear picture in my mind of the route – stone by stone.
> ...
>
> The Stone which measures approx 11 inches by 21 inches is supposed to be resting in its original seating of marble, but [I] presume half of it is missing. The Stone so far as I can make out resembles a well filled pillo...Having seen it and sat on it, I have no doubts about it being the real thing.

In a third letter, he gives his pedigree to emphasise his right to know the secret of the Stone of Destiny, and he quotes from a document found in the ancient chest, said to date from 1720. His letters have been scrutinised by experts at Register House in Edinburgh, and by the Clan Donald Centre in Armadale. They concluded that the document from the chest was unlikely to be genuine, at least in its date of 1720, and they noted that the family tree he quoted was faulty, and that he did not appear to be related to the Macdonalds of Sleat.

The credibility of the story of the Skye Stone was given a huge boost in the 1970s by the publication of Nigel Tranter's trilogy about Robert the Bruce. However, in the half century since then, many walkers, antiquarians, explorers and other interested individuals have tramped the hillsides of Sleat, and investigated its waterfalls and caves, but nothing has ever been found. Furthermore, the chest, said to have been in the ownership of C Iain Alastair Macdonald, has never been produced.

Moncreiffe Hill

If the monks of Scone Abbey did exchange a block of Old Red Sandstone for the Stone of Destiny, they would have had to find somewhere to hide the original stone. They may have thought that hiding it in a discrete cave or concealed chamber would be more suitable than burying it on site in the Abbey grounds. There are two strong traditions which fill this conceptual void, but sadly little concrete evidence to corroborate either.

The first is that the Stone of Destiny was hidden on Moncreiffe Hill. Moncreiffe Hill is a modest ridge of low hills overlooking the River Tay as it pierces the gap between the Ochil range and the Sidlaw Hills, to enter the Carse of Gowrie and flow towards the North Sea. At the eastern end of the ridge is the Moredun Top on which was an important Iron-Age hill fort during the first millennium BC. It has a commanding view of the Tay from Scone to Dundee, and also of the River Earn as it makes its way to its junction with the Tay. The tradition is that the Stone of Destiny was floated down the river and hidden in a cave on the hillside. Then the entrance to the cave was either blocked to conceal it, or obscured by a landslip, and its location has been lost and the Stone of Destiny has never been discovered.

Dunsinane Hill

A somewhat stronger tradition pertains to Dunsinane Hill which is a prominent hilltop in the centre of the Sidlaw range around 7 miles (as the crow flies) from Scone. It provides extensive views to the Tay and over Strathmore. On its summit is one of the most spectacular Iron-Age hill top defensive sites in the region, dating from the first millennium BC, and possibly still occupied in the eleventh century, at the time of Macbeth.

Dunsinane fort consisted of a massive citadel on the summit of the hill surrounded by a very substantial drystone wall and two outer ramparts. Below the citadel, but within the drystone wall, were more extensive constructions which are now believed to have been domestic buildings.

The legends that have sprung up about Dunsinane Hill involve a heady mix of pure fiction, myth and mystery, but there are some established facts. Dunsinane Hill came suddenly to the attention of the Scottish, and indeed the British, public on the 1st of January 1819, when the following letter was published in The Times, and republished over the next few days in several other newspapers including the *Morning Chronicle* and the *Glasgow Herald*. None of the letters was signed, and the author has never been identified. Additionally, the 'two round tablets' detailed in the letter generated little comment.

MacBeth's Castle (Curious Discovery):

On the 19th of November, as the servants belonging to the West Mains of Dunsinane house were employed carrying away stones from the excavation made among the ruins that point out the site of MacBeth's castle, part of the ground they stood on suddenly gave way, and sank down about six feet, discovering a regular vault, about six feet long and four feet wide. None of the men being injured, curiosity induced them to clear out the subterranean recess, when they discovered among the ruins a large stone weighing about 500 lbs, which is pronounced to be of the meteoric or semi-metallic kind. This stone must have lain here during the long series of ages since MacBeth's reign.

Beside it were also found two round tablets of a composition resembling bronze. On one of these two lines are engraved, which a gentleman has thus deciphered – 'The sconce (or shadow) of kingdom come, until sylphs in air carry me again to Bethel'. These plates exhibit the figures of targets for the arms. From time immemorial it has been believed among us here, that unseen hands brought Jacob's pillow from Bethel, and dropped it on the site where the palace of Scoon now stands A strong belief is also entertained by many in this part of the country that it was only a representation of this Jacob's pillow that Edward sent to Westminster, the sacred stone not having been found by him. The curious here, aware of such traditions, and who have viewed these venerable remains of antiquity, agree that MacBeth may, or rather must, have deposited the stone in question at the bottom of his Castle, on the hill of Dunsinane (from the trouble of the times), where it has been found by the workmen.

This curious stone has been shipped for London for the inspection of the scientific amateur, in order to discover its real quality.

155

Seton Gordon, the noted Scottish photographer, naturalist and folk-lorist, writing in 1948 in his book, *Highways and Byways of the Central Highlands*, recounts a similar local tradition which he was told had been handed down through several generations. It was related to him by the Earl of Mansfield, who said that 'somewhere around the dates 1795–1820', two farm workers were walking across Dunsinane Hill and were caught in a torrential downpour, which had caused a small landslip, and which had revealed:

> a fissure which seemed to penetrate deep into the hillside. They explored the fissure and came at last to the broken wall of a subterranean chamber. In one corner of the chamber was a stair which was blocked with debris, and in the centre of the chamber they saw a slab of stone covered with hieroglyphics, and supported by four short stone legs. As there was no evidence of "treasure" the two men did not realise the importance of their "find" and did not talk of what they had seen.

The Stone of Destiny!

Apparently, the lads knew nothing of the legends that either Macbeth or the monks of Scone Abbey had secreted the Stone of Destiny in Dunsinane Hill, and they did not realise the potential importance of their find. The story only emerged later, following the letter in *The Times*, but when people went searching for the fissure, of course, they could not find it. It is possible, perhaps likely, that the ultimate source of Seton Gordon's 'tradition' was *The Times* letter.

Surprisingly, there is no record that either the stone or the 'tablets' were removed from the 'subterranean recess' where they were found, and yet the tablets must have been seen by the 'gentleman' who translated the inscription upon them. Furthermore, they are not mentioned by any of those who reported on subsequent investigations at the site.

At this point, it is important to introduce the confounding element to the story – Shakespeare's play, *The Tragedie of Macbeth*. The heading of the letter to *The Times* (Macbeth's Castle), and several references to Macbeth in the text, including the statement that Macbeth must have deposited the Stone of Destiny 'at the bottom of his castle', demonstrate how the play distorted the history of Macbeth's reign, and gave an entirely fictitious account of his death:

Synopsis of the Play:

In The Tragedie of MacBeth, first performed in 1606, the brave MacBeth fresh from successful battles in support of King Duncan, receives a prophecy from a trio of witches that one day he will become King of Scotland. Consumed by ambition and spurred into action by his wife, MacBeth invites King Duncan to his castle in Inverness, and there murders him and takes the Scottish throne for himself. He is then stricken with guilt, but forced to commit more and more atrocities to protect himself, and he soon becomes a tyrannical ruler.

A second meeting with the witches elicits another prophesy that MacBeth,
...should 'not be afraid of death and bane,
till Birnam Forest shall come to Dunsinane' (Act 5, Scene 3).[2]
and he feels reassured. Forests don't move.

Meanwhile, in Shakespeare's play, Prince Malcolm, Duncan's son, escaped to England, secured the help of the English king, and in due course invaded Scotland with an army of 10,000 men, to challenge MacBeth. At first MacBeth felt secure in his castle on Dunsinane Hill, which Shakespeare tells us, was well defended. However, while camped in Birnam Wood, about 12 miles from Dunsinane Hill, Malcolm's soldiers were ordered to cut down and carry tree branches to camouflage their numbers as they marched towards the castle. MacBeth, on seeing that the witches prophesy had been bypassed, knew he was doomed, but fought on, and was eventually killed and beheaded.

It is well-known that Shakespeare manipulated history, so it is

---

2 Locals pronounce the name Dunsinane to rhyme with 'linen', with the emphasis on the second syllable. Shakespeare's influence ensures that many pronounce it with the emphasis on the last syllable, rhyming with 'rain'.

important to establish the historical facts, and distinguish them from Shakespeare's fiction. Support for King Duncan who had succeeded to the throne in 1034 was concentrated around central Scotland and Perthshire, whereas Macbeth's stronghold was in Moray, a much larger area in the eleventh century than the present county. There is no known evidence that Macbeth had any kind of fortress on Dunsinane Hill.

Macbeth did have a legitimate, if tenuous claim, to the throne of Scotland under the ancient Celtic rules for succession, and was therefore a rival of King Duncan. History, nonetheless, records that it was Duncan, not Macbeth, who initiated the contest for the throne, and in 1040 Duncan led an army into Moray to confront Macbeth. It was, however, Duncan who died in the ensuing battle, perhaps killed by Macbeth himself, and Macbeth succeeded to the throne, and was duly inaugurated on the Stone of Destiny in Scone.

Macbeth reigned for seventeen years, which was quite a long time for a Scottish king of that era, and by all historical accounts it was a peaceful and prosperous period in Scottish history; and Macbeth was considered to be a 'good' king.

By 1057, King Duncan's son, Malcolm, who was only ten years old when Macbeth seized the Crown had, with support from England, raised an army against him, and eventually Macbeth was killed, not in a castle on Dunsinane Hill, but in the Battle of Lumphanan in Aberdeenshire. He was buried in the royal cemetery on Iona.

It is essential to note that all this took place 250 years before Edward I's subjugation of Scotland in 1296 and, moreover, that Macbeth's successor, King Malcolm III (Canmore), was inaugurated in Scone on the Stone of Destiny in 1057. And so the reference in The Times letter to Macbeth secreting the Stone of Destiny on Dunsinane Hill, to secure it 'from the trouble of the times', cannot possibly be historical. The fact that this distortion of Scottish history was not challenged either by the editors of the newspapers who published the story, or publicly by others, emphasises the influence of Shakespeare's play on Scottish history.

It is worth remarking that The Times letter records the fact that there was a long-standing local tradition that the Stone of Destiny was hidden on Dunsinane Hill, although Shakespeare does not mention it in the play. And as we shall see, although it is indeed possible that the Stone of Destiny was concealed on Dunsinane Hill, it was certainly not by Macbeth.

During the early nineteenth century, inspired to a great extent by Shakespeare's Macbeth story, a number of excavations, large and small, were undertaken on Dunsinane Hill. Sadly, none of them was carried out with the scientific rigour of modern investigations. Most of these digs left trails of disturbance which have made subsequent interpretation and analysis much more difficult. Nevertheless, some important discoveries were made. The first of these excavations was carried out in 1799 by James Playfair, at the time the minister of the nearby church of Meigle, and later the Principal of St Andrews University. He cut a trench across the site, and noted how the rampart was founded on rock and built of large stones, but nothing else of significance relating to the Stone of Destiny. His findings were summarised in the *Statistical Accounts of Scotland, 1857*.

In 1854, Mr Nairne of Dunsinane House, at that time the owner of the site, conducted an extensive excavation and made some very interesting discoveries, which were reported to the April 1857 meeting of the Society of Antiquaries of Scotland, by T A Wise FSA Scot:[3]

> Upon digging into the south-east side of the top of the hill, and several feet under the grass covering, four rude chambers were found built of freestone...The stones were undressed and carefully built...These chambers were found to communicate with each other by small passages two feet broad by three feet high.

Further excavation revealed two more chambers:

> ...20 feet in length having two entrances...These chambers had usually a rounded figure, were 7 or 8 feet in diameter, and after the wall height had been raised 2 or 3 feet above the stone flooring, the stones overlapped each other...so as to form a roof which was completed by a flat stone placed over the top, the rude substitute for an arch...Three skulls were found with a number of human bones.

* * *

---

3 *Proceedings of the Society of Antiquaries of Scotland*, Volume II (1857), pp93–99.

Towards the end of the century, David Christison visited the site, and re-examined the results of Nairne's excavation, along with further material and diagrams of the fort contributed by the Dundee historian and archaeologist, Alexander Hutcheson (of whom more below), and others. He reported his conclusions to the Society of Antiquaries of Scotland in 1899.[4] Hutcheson demonstrated that the 'chambers' were not underground caves or excavations, but buildings, probably houses, built on the flat floor of the fort against its outermost wall. He concludes:

> ...that Dunsinane was defended round the top by a dry stone wall...and on the slopes by additional works...and also that it contained much building, the ruins of which, with the accumulated soil of centuries, favoured by burnt timber, of which many traces remained, brought the top to a nearly uniform level, completely burying both wall and buildings; that the evidence of the form and structure of the buildings is contradictory and quite unreliable...

In due course, the whole area was overgrown with grass, and the sward enhanced by the presence of sheep.

It is likely that some of the roofed buildings retained cavities within them, but the careless and inexpert excavations have caused most of them to collapse, leaving hollows and ridges in the turf on the site which can still be seen. In 1927, Alexander Hutcheson (who supplied sketch plans of the site for Christison's report of 1899) reported that he had visited the site, and noted the hollows in the grassy plateau within the wall around the topmost part of the fort where the buildings had been.[5] He was, however, able to enter one of them, although the opening was severely restricted by fallen stones. He confirmed that there were, and no doubt still are, cavities or 'chambers' beneath the grassy turf of Dunsinane Hill. So perhaps the farm workers did not make up the story after all!

* * *

---

4 *Proceedings of the Society of Antiquaries of Scotland* (1899), pp85–93.

5 Alexander Hutcheson, *OLD STORIES IN STONES and Other Papers* (Printed by William Kidd: Dundee, 1927).

One item reported in *The Times* letter which has generated very little comment is the finding of:

> two round tablets, of a composition resembling bronze. On one of these two lines are engraved, which a gentleman has thus deciphered – 'The sconce (or shadow) of kingdom come, until sylphs in air carry me again to Bethel'. These plates exhibit the figures of targets for the arms.

Could the plaques, which are shown on either side of the king on several of the royal seals, for example that of Alexander I, be the bronze tablets referred to in The Times letter? The actual text on the tablet is not recorded, only the translation by 'a gentleman', and it is difficult to make sense of it now. The translation by the 'gentleman' has been translated into Gaelic, and then rendered back to English as, 'Under your protective shadow lies the kingdom until angels carry you back to Bethel'. This relates, of course, to the tradition that the Stone was Jacob's Pillow when he slept at Bethel and dreamt that God would ensure that he would be the father of a great nation. Apart from the farm boys noted in the letter to *The Times*, and presumably, the 'gentleman', no one else has claimed to have seen these tablets. They have been lost, and there is no trace of their whereabouts.

The last sentence of *The Times* letter states that the Stone of Destiny 'has been shipped for London'. For an object of such size and weight, it would have to go by sea, as the roads were not adequate and the railways were still 30 years in the future. Extensive investigations of shipments arriving in London from Scotland, and more particularly of cargoes leaving Perth Harbour, do not list anything that might have been a very large stone.

Notwithstanding the letter claiming it was sent to London, it is possible that the Stone of Destiny did not leave Scotland at all. It may be, in fact, that it did not go very far. D M Hyde, claimed in an article in *The Scots Magazine* in 1954 that he had,

> ascertained locally, beyond reasonable doubt, that the Stone is known to have been taken in the first instance to Bandirran, near Balbeggie, but its subsequent disposal remains a mystery.

This account is corroborated by the recollection of the late Lady Pamela, Countess of Mansfield, who recalled that her father-in-law, the late seventh Earl of Mansfield, told her that the stone had been 'carted away in the 1920s'. It is a remarkable fact that there is no other record that the Stone discovered by the servants from Dunsinane house was ever seen by anyone else, and certainly no account of its removal from the site of its discovery in a chamber on the hillside.

There are two 'Bandirrans' on the OS map, one is a house and the other a nearby farm steading, 'Southtown of Bandirran', both of which are less than a mile southwest of the summit of Dunsinane Hill. Sadly, Hyde does not state when the stone was taken away. Nevertheless, it does seem a little unlikely that the stone, if indeed it was ever removed from the hillside, remained in or around Dunsinane Hill for a hundred years after *The Times* letter, without being mentioned by any of the amateur archaeologists who carried out so many excavations. It is even more unlikely that Dr Wise, reporting on Nairne's findings, would have omitted to mention the stone in his report to the Society of Antiquaries of Scotland if it was there. He did report, as noted by the minister of the nearby Collace Church, that he had found 'a spiral bronze ring in the form of a serpent, the eyes and scales on the back being carved in the most minute manner'. Unfortunately, that ring has been lost.

The tradition that the Stone of Destiny was hidden in Dunsinane Hill certainly predates *The Times* letter, but where the legend originated from, and how far back it goes is difficult to say. Since the Iron-Age fort may have been occupied right up to the eleventh century, it seems certainly possible the monks of Scone would have known that there were old, abandoned buildings within the fort, and, if so, they may have used one of them to conceal the stone.

The Dunsinane mystery continues to resurface from time to time. In 2008, the *Sunday Express* published a series of articles on the Stone of Destiny. In one of them (the 20th of January), the paper reported how a lift engineer who was working in Dunsinane House had heard the owner, Jamie Sinclair, claim that 'He could reach out and touch the Stone of Destiny whenever he wanted'. When challenged by the *Express* reporter he would only say, 'I wouldn't quite go as far as say I would be able to put my hand on it in the next five minutes but, well, it will show up again at some point'.

Remarkably, there has been no significant investigation of the 'chambers' on Dunsinane Hill since 1854. This is surprising given its history, the unverified newspaper reports and the longstanding traditions associated with it. It is difficult to understand why this is so. It is one of the most important hill forts in eastern Scotland; it could be the site where the Stone of Destiny was concealed; and it has literary connections to Shakespeare and Macbeth. What is required is a modern, thoroughly-professional archaeological excavation of the fort on Dunsinane Hill, including not only the remains of defensive constructions on the summit, but the domestic buildings lower down the slope, the results of which might confirm or refute Christison's conclusions that the 'chambers' were domiciles. Experience elsewhere in the world confirms that even where archaeological sites have been looted and seriously damaged, important information can still be gleaned. *Who knows what treasures might be hidden there – the Stone of Destiny?*

It should be noted that there was, in fact, a thorough professional excavation on the site in the summer of 2022, conducted by Professor Gordon Noble of Aberdeen University, but the work was confined to the defensive wall surrounding the summit, and nothing relating to the Stone of Destiny was found.

Summary
Where might the Stone of Destiny have been hidden – the immediate environs of Scone Abbey; the Sleat peninsula on Skye; Moncreiffe Hill; the fort on Dunsinane Hill, or elsewhere near Scone?

It is likely that there would have been two stages in the operation to hide the Stone – the first as Edward's soldiers approached, and secondly if that strategy was successful, a more considered second stage for a more permanent hiding place.

The Stone's considerable weight (*c*200 kg), the need for haste and secrecy as Edward's troops approached, and the necessity to find and in-stall a plausible replacement stone, all ensured that there would be little time to organise transport for any distance. The nearest secure hiding place would be the best, at least for the immediate crisis – perhaps even a crypt beneath the Abbey. If the soldiers, who would not know what the Stone looked like, were deceived about the substitute, they would not be searching for it. Once the soldiers had gone, and the hue and cry had died down, then there would be time to find a secure and secret hiding place.

———————————

Chapter 15
Conclusions

THE OBJECTIVE OF THIS BOOK has been to provide comprehensive accounts of the origin and history of the Stone of Destiny and an engagement with the legends of a Middle Eastern tribe, The Scots, which is claimed to have brought the Stone of Destiny from Spain, and perhaps even the Middle East, to Ireland and thence to Scotland.

A further objective has been to explain how it may have happened that the stone, believed to be the royal inaugural stone associated originally with the Argyllshire dynasty of Kenneth MacAlpin, had been sourced from a seam of sandstone near Scone.

~~~~~~~

Recent evidence from DNA analyses, linguistics and migration studies contradicts the Victorian view, which is still shared by many, that the legends of The Scots were 'nothing but myth and fable'. In fact, it appears that The Scots were a small element of a mass migration of peoples from Scythia (the area north of the Black Sea) to Western Europe, and that they did indeed travel over a period of many centuries from Scythia to Spain, probably via Italy and North Africa, as stated in the Declaration of Arbroath. If that is the case, it corresponds with the folk memory of The Scots and with the accounts in the ancient Scottish and Irish chronicles, so, therefore, they should not be lightly dismissed.

So far as the Stone of Destiny itself is concerned, evidence corroborating the legends is more deficient. However, if it is accepted that the chronicles describing the travels of The Scots from the Middle East, via Galicia, to Ireland and later Argyll are indeed plausible, then credence should also be given to the accounts of the importance to The Scots of an inaugural stone. In this respect, The Scots were not different from neighbouring tribes in the northwest of Spain at that time, which also had royal stones used at inaugurations and when justice was being dispensed.

Both Scottish and Irish legends record that this stone, was brought from Ireland in 500 BC and used at the inauguration of Fergus Mòr mac Eric.

It then became part of the inauguration ceremonies for the subsequent kings of the Scottish Dàl Riada until that of Kenneth MacAlpin in 841. Where exactly these inaugurations took place, however, is unclear. What happened to that stone following MacAlpin's victory over the Picts is one of the defining issue in the debate about Scotland's Stone of Destiny. The conclusion must explain how it is that the Stone of Destiny that we have today is a local piece of Scone sandstone.

There are two possibilities. The first is that MacAlpin abandoned the original stone and adopted in its place a Pictish ceremonial stone in an effort to appease the wounded sentiments of the defeated Picts. This stone was then used for subsequent inaugurations of the Kings of Scots at Scone. The other possibility is that the ancient 'Irish' stone was brought, as the legends record from Argyll to Scone, and then continued to be used for MacAlpin's successors until the inauguration of John Balliol in 1292. Then, when King Edward's soldiers were approaching Scone Abbey in 1296, Abbott Henry and his monks concealed the ancient stone and replaced it with the block of local sandstone that we have today. No other hypotheses have been advanced by historians or antiquarians to explain the conundrum of the local origin of the Stone of Destiny.

In my research for this book, I am struck forcefully by the fact that academic opinion seems united in its view that the reason behind the local (i.e. Scone) origin of the Stone of Destiny is that it was originally a Pictish ceremonial stone, and therefore could have been sourced locally. This view has been put forward strongly by Nick Aitchison. He believes that the Stone of Destiny had been used by the Picts of the Fortriu province of Pictland to inaugurate their kings for generations prior to their defeat by Kenneth MacAlpin and that it was then requisitioned by MacAlpin, and used in all subsequent royal inaugurations at Scone until that of John Balliol in 1292. This is the stone that was returned to Scotland in 1996.

Most academics, including notably the editors of *The Stone of Destiny: Artefact and Icon*, have acquiesced with that view, except for Dauvit Broun and Peter Hill, contributors to the same volume, who appear to be very sceptical. Broun is the first academic, and Hill the first expert, to raise serious doubts in an important academic publication about the Establishment's view that the Stone of Destiny was originally a Pictish inaugural stone which had been requisitioned by Kenneth MacAlpin.

If Aitchison's opinion is substantially correct, then the inevitable corollary is either that The Scots in Argyll never had a ceremonial stone, or that they discarded it when they moved their royal centre from Argyll to Scone. Aitchison's views are contrary to much of the evidence recorded in his book, *Scotland's Stone of Destiny*. He faithfully documents the legends and folk memory which describe a large black, marble or basalt stone, with intricate carvings, and perhaps an inscription, which was brought from Spain (perhaps even from Egypt) first to Ireland, then to Argyll, and finally, by MacAlpin himself to Dunkeld and later to Scone. He, nonetheless, counts these legends as naught, ignoring international experience which has demonstrated the dangers of totally discounting the evidence of legend and folk memory. Furthermore, while he acknowledges the Pictish tradition of exquisite stone carving on objects of cultural or royal significance, he sidesteps the fact that this stone, uniquely, is rough and unadorned save for some crude grooves on its upper surface. And in addition, he offers no explanation to account for its mutilation with iron staples and rings.

If it is accepted that MacAlpin did not requisition an existing royal stone from the defeated Picts and invest it with important ceremonial and, indeed, spiritual qualities, then the Irish Stone of Destiny, having been brought from Argyll, must have continued to play its important role in royal inaugurations right up to 1292, when it was used for the last time for King John Balliol. That this was the case is confirmed by the description by the English cleric, Walter of Guisborough, who described the stone at that inauguration as, 'exceedingly large....and hollowed out as a round chair', and also by studies of the seals of Scotland's mediaeval kings, all of which depict thrones which appear to incorporate a stone which is obviously much larger and heavier, and a different shape from the one removed from Scone Abbey.

It is curious and disappointing that this evidence is not discussed in *The Stone of Destiny: Artefact & Icon*, which investigated so many other aspects relating to the Stone of Destiny. Meanwhile, over the last century, there has been a chorus of historians, archaeologists, journalists and authors of historical novels who have examined the evidence, and have concluded that the Stone of Destiny was indeed substituted by the monks of Scone Abbey, and then concealed somewhere, probably near Scone.

These include Alexander Hutcheson, 1927 ('There were those in Scotland in 1296 quite capable of conveying to safe hiding the royal seat.'); James S Richardson, 1951 ('The Stone removed from Westminster Abbey was not the genuine stone.'); D M Hyde, 1954 ('These facts give strong support to the tradition of substitution in 1296.'); Nigel Tranter, 1960 ('What Edward I took south was just a plain unworked block of Old Red Sandstone'); Janet B Christie, 1970 ('That Edward was duped is clear.'); A C McKerracher, 1984 ('There can be little doubt that Edward had been duped.'); and Pat Gerber, 1997 ('Did Edward realise that the Stone he looted from Scone was not the Stone of Destiny?'). Nevertheless, the academic view continues to favour the *status quo* regarding the Stone of Destiny's history and origin.

In modern times, the Stone of Destiny has been examined officially on three occasions. In none of them was there an answer sought to the question of the possible substitution of the Stone either in 843 by Kenneth MacAlpin, or in 1296 by Abbot Henry. The first examination, in 1952, followed the raid on the Abbey by the Glasgow students, when there was a reasonable concern that the Stone of Destiny may have been copied in Glasgow, and a duplicate deposited in Arbroath Abbey. X-rays taken by the Home Office Scientific Department with portable equipment and without removing the Stone of Destiny from the throne were, understandably, of poor quality, but they revealed the presence of the metal rods inserted by Bailie Gray to repair the broken stone, and its authenticity was confirmed. Until that time, serious doubts about the provenance of the Stone of Destiny were not widespread among historians, and no thoughts about its origins prior to 1296 had been expressed officially, and, consequently, the question of possible substitution was not raised.

Peter Hill, the stone and historic buildings consultant from London who conducted the second official examination of the stone following its return to Edinburgh in 1996, was the first to raise doubts about the established Scottish view that the stone delivered to Edward I was a Pictish royal stone, when he stated in his contribution to *The Stone of Destiny: Artefact & Icon*, that the stone he examined in Edinburgh, 'bears no resemblance whatsoever to known Pictish stonework'. His comments and the implication that the Stone of Destiny is not an ancient Pictish royal stone, are not contradicted nor discussed by the editors of the book.

The third examination by Phillips and his colleagues of the British Geological Survey was conducted in 1998 without removing the Stone from its glass case in the throne room of Edinburgh Castle. Its objective was confined to determining the source seam of Devonian Old Red Sandstone from which the Stone had been quarried. This was done by microscopic geological examination of tiny fragments of the Stone. As noted earlier, it was proved, conclusively, that the Stone of Destiny had been quarried at Kincarrathie, about a mile south of Scone Abbey. Furthermore, since some of the samples examined had been sourced from a previous examination in 1865, it was clear that this indeed was the stone that had lain in Westminster Abbey for 700 years.

Although, by 1996, there was a significant body of opinion that considered that the Stone had been substituted by Abbot Henry, if not by MacAlpin in 843, in none of these examinations was the question of the provenance of the Stone, prior to 1296, part of the objective set by Historic Scotland, nor were comments sought on the possible fate of the ancient 'Irish' Stone, and so no controversial opinions were expressed. Nevertheless, Hill, in the report of his examination and in his comments on ancient Pictish stones, clearly doubted that the Stone of Destiny was originally a Pictish icon, and Broun considered that the ancient Irish stone continued to be used at Scone until 1296.

Notwithstanding the doubts expressed by Hill and Broun, it seems that neither Historic Scotland, nor its successor organisation, Historic Environment Scotland, have been prepared to reconsider the origin of the Stone of Destiny. Nevertheless, it is certain that doubts about the origin of the Stone will not go away, and at the very least they need to be acknowledged.

It is the view of this author that the evidence pointing to the substitution of the Stone of Destiny prior to its transportation down south, while not conclusive, is strong. It is like proving that a murder has been committed without the presence of a body. Until the original Stone of Destiny is found, I am content to quote again, and subscribe to Dauvit Broun's view, that in the aftermath of MacAlpin's takeover of Pictland:

> It may be guessed that the Pictish kingdom lived on in Scone's status as the royal centre of Alba, and that the kingship established by Fergus was represented by the Stone itself.

There are not many heroes associated with the Stone of Destiny. Undoubtedly, Abbot Henry and the monks of Scone Abbey, who braved and perhaps suffered the wrath of Edward I, were Scottish heroes. So also were the six students, Ian Hamilton, Kay Mathieson, Gavin Vernon, Alan Stuart, John Jocelyn and Bill Craig and several prominent Glaswegian individuals, notably Bertie Gray, a Bailie on Glasgow City Council, and John MacCormick, the Lord Rector of Glasgow University, who all risked career-damning criminal convictions, and perhaps prison, had they been apprehended and convicted. But there are not many others. Nor can it be said that there are many villains, apart from the Edward I himself, and perhaps those who ordered the unceremonious return of the Stone of Destiny from Arbroath Abbey. This was done under the cover of darkness, and contrary to promises made by politicians and officials of the Church and State that, if it should be returned, consideration would be given to locating it permanently in Scotland.

Sadly, the original Stone of Destiny has been lost. It may have been concealed somewhere near to Scone Abbey, and if so, it may have been incorporated into the foundations of Scone Palace, or it may have been hidden on Moncreiffe Hill or Dunsinane Hill, elsewhere in Perthshire, or further afield. Undoubtedly, however, it is unlikely that it will be discovered. Nevertheless, the ancient chronicles give us a good idea of what it may have looked like. It was certainly large, considerably larger than the stone plundered by Edward I, and not unlike a Roman altar stone – about 430 mm to 460 mm high and perhaps 380 mm square. It was of a size that would fit into the thrones of Scotland as depicted on the mediaeval royal seals, and tall enough so that it could be sat upon comfortably – especially with a cushion. It is likely that it was black, shiny and marble-like, and the top may have been hollowed out to form a seat. Almost certainly, it was ornately carved.

With the visibility and publicity afforded to the Stone at the Coronation of King Charles III, and with the new Museum of Perth featuring it as its most important attraction, it is right that Scotland should reassess its attitude to the Stone of Destiny. It is time to accept that Scotland has had two Stones of Destiny, and that the one currently on view is the second. Like its predecessor, it represents the continuity and history of the ancient Scots nation and the attachment to the land which that nation occupies.

In that respect it is very appropriate that it came from Scone, at the very heart of the new nation state of Alba created by King Kenneth MacAlpin. Substituted for the ancient Irish stone by Abbott Henry and the monks of Scone Abbey and then taken by force to England, this Stone deserves recognition in its own right. That right is enhanced by its long and controversial history, and should not been diminished by uncertainties about its origin or its rough appearance. It was the object which deceived Edward I of England, the Hammer of the Scots, even in the hour of his greatest glory, and in doing so retained for Scotland an element of pride and dignity at a very dark time in its history.

Silently, for seven centuries it has been a very obvious Scottish presence at the epicentre of power in London. More recently, it was the prize for four daring students in their raid on Westminster Abbey which pricked the high and mighty mystique of the Church and State in London and contributed to the slow re-evaluation of Scotland's relationship to the Union of Parliaments. Now it can be appreciated as Scotland's successor Stone of Destiny, taking over the mantle from its long lost predecessor. At the service for the presentation of the Honours of Scotland to the new King in St Giles Cathedral in the capital city of Scotland, this public recognition was at last granted. Installed in Perth's new museum, it will be accorded the prominence it rightly deserves.

Select Index

Greece 24

Grey, Sir Thomas 17, 52

Greyfriars Church 69, 70

H

Hall, Robin 60

Hamilton, Ian 75–89, 100, 170

Hansard 102, 105

Harry Stanger Ltd 92

Hebrides 3, 12, 27, 35, 44, 151, 152

Hector (Trojan prince) 8

Henrie, David 110

Henry, Abbott 4, 5, 43, 57, 71, 72, 128, 132, 133, 143, 166, 169, 170, 171

Hereditary Bearer of the National Banner of Scotland (Earl of Dundee) 113

Hereditary Bearer of the National Flag of Scotland (Earl of Lauderdale) 113

Hibernia 20

High King of Ireland 30, 31

Highland Safaris 94

Highways and Byways of the Central Highlands 156

Hill of Tara 22, 24, 27, 30, 31, 33, 40

Hill, Peter 110, 134, 145, 149, 166, 168

Hitler, Adolf 100

Historic Scotland 94, 110, 119, 128, 136, 138, 144, 169

Historic Environment Scotland 9, 169

History of Scotland by Walter Scott 22

Holy Oil 71, 72

Holyrood Palace 112

Homecoming 91, 117, 118

Honours of Scotland 3, 12, 106, 114, 115 117, 132, 133, 171

House of Commons 85, 88, 99, 101, 102, 105, 107

House of Lords 101, 102

Hughes, Emrys (MP) 102

Hundred Years War 66

Hunterian Museum 53

Huntingtower 150

Hutcheson, Alexander 160, 168

Hyber 20

Hyde D M 161, 162, 168

Hymer 20

I

Iberia 2, 24, 41

Icolmkyll 32

India 152, 153

Inspector of Ancient Monuments of Scotland. *See* James S Richardson

Iona 2, 31–35, 37, 54, 55, 56, 69, 125, 142, 152, 158

Ireland 2, 4, 12, 14, 18, 20–31, 33, 34, 36, 37, 40, 43, 53, 56, 100, 101, 125, 128, 131, 136, 138, 141–144, 149, 165, 167

Irish 4, 13, 22–35, 40, 41, 52, 82, 91, 100, 101, 137, 139, 142, 165, 166, 167, 169, 171

Irish Sea 30

Irish Home Rule Bills 101

Morris, Andrew 125
Mortimer, Roger 64, 65
Moses (Biblical character) 1, 18–22, 40
Mull 12, 30, 34
Munro, Graeme 128, 138
Munro, Neil 101
Murray, Alex 92

Murray, Arthur George. *See* Viscount Elibank
Murray, David, 3rd Earl of Mansfield 150
Murtagh mac Eric 30, 31
myth 11, 13, 18, 40, 41, 63, 129, 130, 165

N

Mr Nairne (Dunsinane House) 159
National Museum of Scotland 110, 117, 145
Nazis 100
Neville's Cross (Battle of) 66
Newcastle (HMS) 114
New Testament 113
Niall of the Nine Hostages 33
Nimmo, John MacKay 90, 91, 93
Niul 19
Noble, Gordon (Professor) 163
Norham 60
North Africa 2, 18, 23, 25, 26, 165
North Channel 2, 27
North Wind of Love 123
Northumberland 12, 61, 109
Norway 25, 45, 56, 59, 60
No Stone Unturned 75

O

Oban 2, 12, 28, 136, 141, 142
O'Byrne, John Patrick 103, 111
Ochil Hills 39, 154
Oengus (King) 145
Ogg, Angus (MacDonald) 151, 152
Old Scone 1, 137
Old Testament 1, 15
Oliver Cromwell 4, 100
origin myth 130
Orkney 11 (map) 60
Orygynale Cronykil 17
Ossian 1
Our Descent from Israel 16

P

Para Handy 101
Perth 5, 39, 61, 63, 73, 92, 107, 108, 117–121, 132, 136, 142, 146, 152, 161, 170, 171
Perth 800th anniversary 218
Perth & Kinross Council 118, 120
Perth Market Place Ltd 120
Perth City Hall 5, 119, 120
Perth Museum 1, 5, 107, 118–121
Perthshire 1, 3, 5, 12, 37, 38, 56, 83, 108, 120 ,126, 158, 170
Pharaoh 2, 18, 19

Philip IV of France (King) 61, 66

Phillips, Emrys 139, 141, 142

Pictish Chronicle 37

Pictland 3, 11, 12, 33, 38, 56, 145, 149, 166, 169

Picts 3, 4, 12, 13, 28, 30, 34, 37, 52, 56, 128, 130, 143–146

Pillars of Hercules 14, 23

Playfair, James 158

Pliny 20

Pocock, Richard (Bishop) 141

Poets' Corner 77, 78

Pope 13, 14, 15, 71, 72

Private Members Bill 102

Processus 13, 14

Ptolemy 20

Q

Quarrymill 136, 138

Queensferry 49

R

Ramsay, Sir Andrew 141

Randolph, Thomas 151

Red Sea 14, 19

Reformation 117, 121, 137, 150

Register House 153

Rerum Scoticarum Historiae 44

Richardson, James S 47, 48, 49, 51, 53, 133, 134, 168

River Add 3, 35

Robbie the Pict 106, 126

Rochester 79, 84

Rollo, John 84

Roman altar stone 51, 53, 54, 170

Romans 12, 54

Rome 69, 70, 71, 72, 145

Romania 2, 14, 15, 25

Ross Herald 112

Rothesay Herald 112

Russia 15, 25, 26

Russian Federation 2

Rutherford, Adam 99

S

St Adomnàn 32, 55

St Andrew 15

St Andrews 145, 159

St Andrews Cathedral 13, 145

St Andrew's Day 5, 46, 61, 105, 111, 112, 123, 130

St Boniface 52

St Columba 2, 31–35, 37, 52, 54, 55, 56, 90, 91, 94, 125

St Columba's Church (Dundee) 90, 91

St Cumine the White 32, 55

St Giles Cathedral 106, 112–115

St John's Kirk 5, 107, 119, 121

St Màol-Rubha 31, 91

St Ninian 52

St Serf's Priory 17

St Vigeans 135

Sarcophagus (St Andrews) 145

OTHER TITLES FROM TIPPERMUIR BOOKS

Spanish Thermopylae (2009)

Battleground Perthshire (2009)

Perth: Street by Street (2012)

Born in Perthshire (2012)

In Spain with Orwell (2013)

Trust (2014)

Perth: As Others Saw Us (2014)

Love All (2015)

A Chocolate Soldier (2016)

The Early Photographers of Perthshire (2016)

Taking Detective Novels Seriously: The Collected Crime Reviews of Dorothy L Sayers (2017)

Walking with Ghosts (2017)

No Fair City: Dark Tales from Perth's Past (2017)

The Tale o the Wee Mowdie that wantit tae ken wha keeched on his heid (2017)

Hunters: Wee Stories from the Crescent: A Reminiscence of Perth's Hunter Crescent (2017)

A Little Book of Carol's (2018)

Flipstones (2018)

Perth: Scott's Fair City: The Fair Maid of Perth & Sir Walter Scott – A Celebration & Guided Tour (2018)

God, Hitler, and Lord Peter Wimsey: Selected Essays, Speeches and Articles by Dorothy L Sayers (2019)

Perth & Kinross: A Pocket Miscellany: A Companion for Visitors and Residents (2019)

The Piper of Tobruk: Pipe Major Robert Roy, MBE, DCM (2019)

The 'Gig Docter o Athole': Dr William Irvine & The Irvine Memorial Hospital (2019)

Afore the Highlands: The Jacobites in Perth, 1715–16 (2019)

'Where Sky and Summit Meet': Flight Over Perthshire – A History: Tales of Pilots, Airfields, Aeronautical Feats, & War (2019)

Diverted Traffic (2020)

Authentic Democracy: An Ethical Justification of Anarchism (2020)

'If Rivers Could Sing': A Scottish River Wildlife Journey. A Year in the Life of the River Devon as it flows through the Counties of Perthshire, Kinross-shire & Clackmannanshire (2020)

A Squatter o Bairnrhymes (2020)

In a Sma Room Songbook: From the Poems by William Soutar (2020)

The Nicht Afore Christmas: the much-loved yuletide tale in Scots (2020)

Ice Cold Blood (2021)

The Perth Riverside Nursery & Beyond: A Spirit of Enterprise and Improvement (2021)

Fatal Duty: The Scottish Police Force to 1952: Cop Killers, Killer Cops & More (2021)

The Shanter Legacy: The Search for the Grey Mare's Tail (2021)

'Dying to Live': The Story of Grant McIntyre, Covid's Sickest Patient (2021)

The Black Watch and the Great War (2021)

Beyond the Swelkie: A Collection of Poems & Writings to Mark the Centenary of George Mackay Brown (2021)

Sweet F.A. (2022)

A War of Two Halves (2022)

A Scottish Wildlife Odyssey (2022)

In the Shadow of Piper Alpha (2022)

Mind the Links: Golf Memories (2022)

Perthshire 101: A Poetic Gazetteer of the Big County (2022)

The Banes o the Turas: An Owersettin in Scots o the Poems bi Pino Mereu scrievit in Tribute tae Hamish Henderson (2022)

Walking the Antonine Wall: A Journey from East to West Scotland (2022)

The Japan Lights: On the Trail of the Scot Who Lit Up Japan's Coast (2023)

Fat Girl Best Friend: 'Claiming Our Space' – Plus Size Women in Film & Television (2023)

Wild Quest Britain: A Nature Journey of Discovery through England, Scotland & Wales – from Lizard Point to Dunnet Head (2023)

Guid Mornin! Guid Nicht! (2023)

Madainn Mhath! Oidhche Mhath! (2023)

Who's Aldo? (2023)

FORTHCOMING

The Mysterious Case of the Stone of Destiny: A Scottish Historical Detective Whodunnit! (David Maule, 2024)

A History of Irish Republicanism in Dundee (c1840 to 1985) (Rùt Nic Foirbeis, 2024)

William Soutar: Collected Poetry, Volumes I & II (Published Work) (Paul S Philippou (Editor-in-Chief) & Kirsteen McCue and Philippa Osmond-Williams (editors), 2024)

William Soutar: Complete Poetry, Volume III (Miscellaneous & Unpublished Poetry) (Paul S Philippou (Editor-in-Chief) & Kirsteen McCue and Philippa Osmond-Williams (editors), 2025)

William Soutar: Complete Poetry, Volume IV (Prose Selections) (Paul S Philippou (Editor-in-Chief) & Kirsteen McCue and Philippa Osmond-Williams (editors), 2026)

The Whole Damn Town (Hannah Ballantyne, 2024)

Balkan Rhapsody (Maria Kassimova-Moisset, translated by Iliyana Nedkova Byrne, 2024)

The Black Watch from the Crimean War to the Second Boer War (Derek Patrick and Fraser Brown, 2024)

All Tippermuir Books titles are available from bookshops and online booksellers. They can also be purchased directly (with free postage & packing (UK only) – minimum charges for overseas delivery) from **www.tippermuirbooks.co.uk**.